Subprime Mortgages

Also of interest from the Urban Institute Press:

Private Neighborhoods and the Transformation of Local Government,
by Robert H. Nelson

A Primer on U.S. Housing Markets and Housing Policy,
by Richard K. Green and Stephen Malpezzi

*Choosing a Better Life? Evaluating the Moving to Opportunity Social
Experiment,* edited by John Goering and Judith D. Feins

Clearing the Way: Deconcentrating the Poor in Urban America,
by Edward G. Goetz

Subprime Mortgages

America's Latest Boom and Bust

Edward M. Gramlich

THE URBAN INSTITUTE PRESS
Washington, D.C.

THE URBAN INSTITUTE PRESS
2100 M Street, N.W.
Washington, D.C. 20037

Library of Congress Cataloging-in-Publication Data

Gramlich, Edward M.
   Subprime mortgages : America's latest boom and bust / Edward M. Gramlich
        p. cm.
   Includes bibliographical references and index.
   ISBN 978-0-87766-739-1 (alk. paper)
   1.   Mortgage loans—United States.   I. Title.
   HG2040.5.U5G73   2007
   332.7'22—dc22

                                        2007017806

Printed in the United States of America

10 09 08 07   1 2 3 4 5

THE URBAN INSTITUTE is a nonprofit, nonpartisan policy research and educational organization established in Washington, D.C., in 1968. Its staff investigates the social, economic, and governance problems confronting the nation and evaluates the public and private means to alleviate them. The Institute disseminates its research findings through publications, its web site, the media, seminars, and forums.

Through work that ranges from broad conceptual studies to administrative and technical assistance, Institute researchers contribute to the stock of knowledge available to guide decisionmaking in the public interest.

Conclusions or opinions expressed in Institute publications are those of the authors and do not necessarily reflect the views of officers or trustees of the Institute, advisory groups, or any organizations that provide financial support to the Institute.

For Ruth, who fought for me passionately.

Contents

Foreword

The troubles in the subprime mortgage market came to the public's attention as this book was being written. Accounts of high foreclosure rates among borrowers who took out unconventional mortgages and insolvency among some lenders followed earlier reports of predatory lending practices and regulatory incongruities between prime and subprime mortgages. With his experience as a former governor of the Federal Reserve and board chair of the Neighborhood Reinvestment Corporation and his expertise as one of the nation's leading economists, Dr. Gramlich is uniquely qualified to provide a balanced analysis of this relatively new market.

However perilous the new home-financing world that Dr. Gramlich describes, it also offers opportunity to many whose financial or personal circumstances previously precluded them from homeownership. True, a quarter of unconventional mortgages end up in default. But, as Gramlich stresses, the three-quarters that don't are taken out by households that probably couldn't have received a traditional mortgage. For this group, high risks may justify high costs—*if* these costs are fair and well understood by borrowers.

The policy recommendations that Dr. Gramlich spells out would reform and strengthen the subprime market so it better serves borrowers, honest lenders, and investors in mortgages. These recommendations pass three key tests. They are incremental, so current administrative and regulatory systems don't have to be junked to right this new and important segment of the mortgage industry. They speak to an issue—home owning—that isn't the property of a single political party. And they are numerous, so progress can be made on many fronts at once and a winning combination of policies can be cobbled together. A policy trifecta like this doesn't come along often.

That said, the same developments that are already validating Dr. Gramlich's explanation of why casualties among buyers and lenders were inevitable aren't self-correcting, so it's essential to consider the fixes proposed here very seriously and very soon. Even if the problems in the subprime mortgage market aren't likely to trigger significant damage to the overall housing market, the goal of home owning could be put out of the reach of millions of mostly low-income families if reforms, such as those proposed by Dr. Gramlich, are not implemented soon.

Robert D. Reischauer
President, The Urban Institute

Acknowledgments

When I arrived as a new governor of the Federal Reserve Board in November 1997, Chairman Alan Greenspan asked me which committee I would like to serve on. I investigated and chose the Committee on Consumer and Community Affairs as its work interested me the most. Given personnel shifts, I soon became chair of the committee and continued in that position until I left the Board in 2005. As an ex officio extension of duties, I also headed the Board's public-member Consumer Affairs Committee and served on the Board of the Neighborhood Reinvestment Corporation, now NeighborWorks America, chairing that board for four years.

All these positions exposed me to an issue I had not been aware of, America's low-income housing problems. I have now participated in hours and hours of discussion of the problems, the good things that are happening (and there are many), the bad things, and the potential solutions. Over these years, I gave many speeches on the topic. For most of my time at the Fed, I kept challenging other economists—"This is interesting; you ought to write it up." They didn't, so I have now tried. The result is this book.

I have been helped by many, many people. First, I would like to thank Robert Reischauer and others at the Urban Institute who make it incredibly easy to publish monographs. In particular, late in the preparation of this manuscript, I became ill and had to rely heavily on Kathleen Courrier,

Eugene Steuerle, and Margery Austin Turner to help me finish the job. Henry Chen was a marvelously competent research assistant who did most of the statistical work, and Daniel Kuehn created most of the charts. Karen Smith guided Henry and me through the Urban Institute's Dynasim model, and Christopher Hayes and Elizabeth Guernsey ran tabulations of mortgage data.

I drew liberally on my old colleagues at the Fed. My main tutors on mortgage markets there (and often my speechwriters) were Glenn Canner and Robert Avery. They took many questions and discussed my policy ideas. Andreas Lehnert offered comments, and Kevin Moore helped me navigate the Survey of Consumer Finances. Rebecca Tsangare and Sean Wallace were also skilled in supplying yet more mortgage data.

On the Fed's consumer side, Sandy Braunstein has been an invaluable source of discussion, as has been James Michaels on many legal aspects. For community reinvestment, my sources have been Glenn Loney and Dan Sokolov.

While at the Fed I made many road trips for NeighborWorks America. I benefited from discussions with people up and down this highly skilled organization, particularly George Knight, Ellen Lazar, Kenneth Wade, and Bruce Gottschall.

Financial support for the project has come from the Ford Foundation, the Fannie Mae Foundation, and Freddie Mac. To each group I express the hope that the book lives up to expectations.

1

The New Mortgage Market

Right after World War II, the American economy saw a major increase in homeownership. The overall homeownership rate rose from 45 to 65 percent in little more than a decade. This first ownership boom was characterized by the opening up of mortgage credit and ownership possibilities to the middle class. Millions of these middle-class households took advantage of newly available long-term, fixed-rate mortgages to buy houses, generally in the suburbs. These families moved out of the cities, purchased split-level houses, set up their backyard swing-sets, and placed their children in suburban public schools.

Low- and moderate-income families generally were unable to participate in this first postwar ownership boom. Many of them could not get mortgage credit at all; those that could, could not afford either the standard 20-percent down payment or the monthly payments. Minority families often could not participate because they faced discrimination on top of these other factors. By and large these families remained in rental housing. After its burst in the 1950s, America's overall homeownership rate stayed close to 65 percent for another 35 years.

But lately there has been another, albeit smaller, ownership boom. As recently as 1994, America's overall ownership rate was stable at 64 percent. But by 2005, it had risen to 69 percent (figure 1.1). Comparing earlier and later population sizes and ownership rates, nearly 12 million American households became new homeowners over this 11-year period. Like their

Figure 1.1. Homeownership Rates, 1940–2005

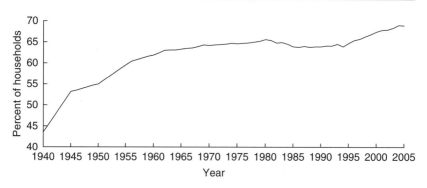

Source: U.S. Census Bureau data.

middle-class cohorts in earlier years, these new homeowners now have a chance to build wealth, invest in their neighborhoods, send their children to better schools, and reap the other advantages of ownership. The latest increase moves the United States into the top rung in world homeownership rates. It has been the subject of intense cheering from presidents Clinton and Bush, though the federal deficit problem has been sufficiently constraining that most of this cheering has come from the bully pulpit, not in the form of new federal money.

The earlier homeownership boom focused on the middle classes and the prime mortgage market. These prime borrowers took out long-term mortgages, secured by their homes, generally for 30 years. They paid mortgage rates of around 6 percent, and their mortgages covered 80 or 90 percent of their home price. The new ownership boom has moved one step down the income scale, focusing largely (though not exclusively) on the so-called subprime market. Subprime borrowers generally have lower incomes and often are not able to put as much down—their loan-to-value ratios often go up to 100 percent. Because of their worse credit history, subprime borrowers have to pay much higher interest rates, points, and fees, and they normally must accept prepayment penalties to get their home-secured loans. When the points and fees are amortized, the effective mortgage rate, called the average percentage rate (APR), is often in the double digits.

With rates this high, and with continuing pressures to expand ownership, people have been tempted to stretch the limits. Borrowers have sought ways to get in a house by keeping their down payments and monthly payments as low as possible. Lenders have sought new business. The combination has led to shortcuts that can often cause problems—excessive reliance on adjustable rate mortgages (ARMs), not verifying the repayment ability of the borrower, or not escrowing taxes and insurance payments. The mortgage of choice in this new subprime market is known as the 2/28—the interest rate is fixed rate for 2 years, and then for the rest of the 28 years the loan becomes an ARM. Sometimes this mortgage is varied to a 3/27, which works essentially the same way. Other types of "nontraditional" mortgage products, such as interest-only mortgages and negative-amortization mortgages, have also come into increasing use.[1]

While all income groups have participated in this new opening up of the mortgage market and rise in homeownership, low- and moderate-income households and racial and ethnic minorities have been at the center of the boom. From 1994 to 2005, the overall ownership rate rose from 64 to 69 percent. The rate for blacks rose from 42 to 49 percent, a rise that contributed to the increase of nearly 1.5 million black homeowners over the period. The rate for Hispanics went from 42 to 50 percent, accounting for many of the 2 million additional Hispanic homeowners (figure 1.2). The rate for households indicating more than one race rose from 52 to 60 percent, helping to add another 2 million homeowners. The rate for homeowners in the lowest tenth of the income distribution rose from 39 to

Figure 1.2. Homeownership Rates by Race or Ethnicity, 1970–2005

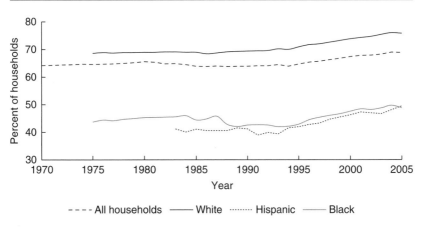

Source: U.S. Census Bureau data.

43 percent, in the second tenth from 45 to 49 percent, and so forth. An unusual number of all these groups is first-time homebuyers.

The subprime mortgage market developed for several reasons, essentially the material of chapter 2. One important factor was the Depository Institutions Deregulatory and Monetary Control Act of 1980. This act effectively abolished usury laws on first-lien mortgages. Usury laws, which prevent mortgages above a certain rate from even being made, acted to shut low- and moderate-income borrowers out of credit markets. As these usury laws passed from the scene, instead of denying mortgage credit, mortgage lenders could now make loans, though with higher interest rates to conform to the worse credit prospects of the new borrowers. It took a while for this change to take effect, but lately there has been a noticeable drop in mortgage denial rates (figure 1.3).

There were other factors. The 1990s saw the development and refinement of automated techniques for approving credit applications. Lenders now use credit scoring and similar techniques much more often than earlier, in the mortgage market and in other credit markets, leading to a faster and more inclusive mechanism for generating mortgage approvals. Some lenders now make mortgage approvals in a few minutes. Many old-line lenders such as banks and thrifts have set up subprime mortgage affiliates to make loans in the new part of the mortgage market. The 1990s saw the advent of mortgage brokers, intermediaries between

Figure 1.3. Denial Rates for Conventional Mortgages by Race and Income, 1997–2005

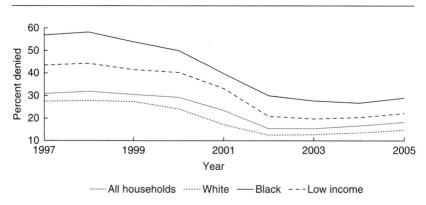

Source: Home Mortgage Disclosure Act data, 2005.

lenders and borrowers, who are open, in the neighborhood, and available to place mortgages for a fee.

The influence of capital markets has played a significant role in the development of the subprime mortgage market. Fannie Mae and Freddie Mac, huge secondary market mortgage entities, began securitizing prime mortgages in the 1970s. By the 1990s, private Wall Street markets were doing it in the subprime market, introducing huge new sources of capital and financing largely unsupervised subprime mortgage lenders. Many of the latest problems have occurred because of the lack of careful lender supervision in this sector of the market.

On the nonprofit side of the ledger, there was also a substantial increase in community-based organizations (CBOs). These CBOs receive funds to subsidize affordable mortgages and make them to low- and moderate-income groups. Groups including NeighborWorks America (NWA) and the Opportunity Finance Network (OFN) have organized many local CBOs into vigorous and effective national networks.

Government regulations have had an impact as well. One that is particularly important is the Community Reinvestment Act (CRA), which gives banks and thrifts a responsibility to plow back funds to low- and moderate-income borrowers in their business areas, called assessment areas. CRA was first passed back in 1977, over the strong objections of the banks. But now, banks have made many low- and moderate-income mortgages to fulfill their CRA obligations, they have found default rates pleasantly low, and they generally charge low mortgages rates. Thirty years later, CRA lending has become a very good business (Gramlich 1999).[2]

Yet another factor has been the economy itself. Recessions have been less severe and frequent in recent decades; in fact, there were only two between 1982 and 2006, and they were relatively mild. Meanwhile, the continual dampening of inflation in the 1980s and early 1990s eventually translated to lower nominal interest rates (both long-term and short-term). The combination of more stable employment and lower payments to support a mortgage created ideal economic conditions for expansion of the mortgage market.

One factor that does *not* seem to have influenced the growth in the subprime market much is a factor common for housing and mortgages in general, the well-known income tax preferences for housing—both the deductions for mortgage interest and property taxes and the generous treatment of capital gains on houses. The deductions for interest and taxes are unlikely to matter much because most low- and moderate-income homeowners do not itemize deductions. The generous capital gains treatment may not matter much either for households that are not paying a large amount in income taxes.

Reflecting all these positive factors, back in 1994 subprime mortgage originations were $35 billion, less than 5 percent of total mortgage originations. By 2005 subprime mortgage originations had risen to $625 billion, 20 percent of total originations (figure 1.4). This works out to a whopping 26 percent annual rate of increase over the whole decade. From being essentially nonexistent back in 1994, subprime mortgages are now 7 percent of the total mortgage stock. The subprime market was barely known in 1994, but merely a decade later, it is a huge factor. And the prime mortgage market expanded as well, again to accommodate the new loan demand emanating from all households, again including those low- and moderate-income households and racial minorities who could qualify for prime loans.

While it seems highly desirable to open up mortgage markets to these new borrowers, often for the first time, any major social movement on this scale will likely have drawbacks. And there are drawbacks associated with the subprime mortgage market. A first is simply its novelty. The subprime market opened for the first time, and as described above, an unusual share of the new mortgages were nontraditional products that featured adjustable rates. Short-term interest rates were very low in this period, for good macroeconomic reasons, and the initial cost of these new subprime mortgages was low. In addition, many lenders treated the two-year rate as a

Figure 1.4. Mortgage Originations by Type of Mortgage, 1994–2005 (billions of dollars)

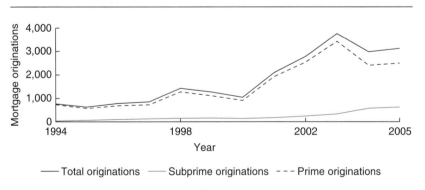

Source: Home Mortgage Disclosure Act data, 2005.

teaser and advertised on this basis. Now that short-term rates have returned to more realistic (higher) levels, many subprime borrowers are suffering large payment shocks.

Further, house prices have been rising smartly in many local markets, permitting many borrowers who may have gotten in trouble on their mortgage to sell the house, pay the prepayment penalty, and walk away from the whole deal without much loss. But this period is ending too. House price increases began to slack off in 2006. Because of the rise in short-term rates, combined with reduced house price appreciation, the new subprime mortgage market is now being stress-tested in a major way.

There are added complications. While the prime mortgage market is well regulated and supervised, with the major lenders—banks and thrifts—undergoing arduous examinations every three years, the subprime market is much less so. All mortgage markets operate under general federal statutes preventing discrimination, insuring proper disclosures, and regulating other aspects of mortgage transactions. But in the subprime market, 30 percent of the loans are made by subsidiaries of banks and thrifts, less tightly supervised than their parent company, and 50 percent are made by independent mortgage companies, state-chartered but not subject to much federal supervision at all.[3] Mortgage brokers are largely unsupervised, with minimal incentives to see that borrowers get their best deal and only indirect incentives to see that borrowers will be able to make their mortgage payments. And many subprime borrowers are from lower-income households, not well-versed in financial matters and vulnerable to losses in income or payment ability.

The consequence of all these factors is that many borrowers could fall behind on their mortgage payments and go into delinquency status, sometimes even getting foreclosed on their loans. In a foreclosure, a borrower's house is taken away and the borrower has to move out, typically losing any equity that has been accumulated in the house in the process. Foreclosures have never been much of a problem in the prime mortgage market, with overall foreclosure rates staying below 1 percent for many years. In the subprime market, by contrast, they *have been* about ten times as high, more like 7 percent (Joint Center for Housing Studies 2006, figure 25). And what happens now that short-term interest rates have risen and house price increases have slacked off is anyone's guess. The Center for Responsible Lending (CRL), having studied 6 million recent subprime mortgages, predicts a sharp increase in foreclosure rates, up to 20 percent for newly made subprime loans (Schloemer et al. 2006).

There are problems on the other side of the market too. By February 2007, the *Wall Street Journal* reported that at least 20 subprime lenders had filed for bankruptcy, with more likely to follow.[4] On April 2 they were joined by New Century Financial, the third-largest subprime lender in 2005 and a poster child for the go-go subprime market. A bond index fund that registers investors' expectation that the value of low-rated subprime mortgage bonds will fail lost 30 percent of its value in the first two months of 2007.[5]

A mortgage foreclosure is the dramatic culmination of a process. But for every mortgage that is foreclosed, many others are very near foreclosure. A household may be struggling to make payments and in a situation where if the least little thing goes wrong, the household will fall behind. Things that could go wrong include loss of a job, a health problem (many of these families are among the 45 million Americans now without health insurance), or a problem with the house itself, such as a leaky roof.

There are indications that these pre-foreclosure issues may be serious as well. According to macroeconomic data, personal saving rates are negative and consumer debt burdens and personal bankruptcies are at all-time highs.[6] Studies of longitudinal income data indicate that about 40 percent of first-time low-income homebuyers go back to renting after their first homeowning experience. It is not clear why, but this share is much higher than for other higher-income new homeowning groups, leading to the suspicion that many low-income homeowners are making distress sales (Herbert and Belsky 2006, chapter 3). Further studies from panel data indicate that the volatility of income flows for low- and moderate-income households has increased from earlier decades (Hacker 2006). And there are other ways in which households are now subject to increased risk. Putting this all together, the CRL estimates that another 5 to 10 percent of recent subprime mortgages are likely to be resolved by distress prepayments (Schloemer et al. 2006).

When something does go wrong, or even if it does not, the family may be at the mercy of predatory lenders, a group that often takes advantage of low-income, less-literate, less financially savvy, and more vulnerable borrowers. Such terms as asset-based lending (lending on the basis of the value of an asset in a foreclosure proceeding, not on the loan payment prospects), loan-flipping (rapid refinance of mortgages often without cause, but with big closing costs), equity-stripping (losing the equity in one's house), and outright fraud and abuse have colored the foreclosure discussions (Renuart 2004; Goldstein 2007).

So there it is. There is both good news and bad news in the opening up of the mortgage market, particularly the subprime market. The good news is that millions of new homeowners, who formerly would have been denied mortgage credit, can now take out mortgage loans, buy homes, live in better neighborhoods, and send their kids to better schools. A great many of these new homeowners, most likely a majority, are making their mortgage payments on schedule and building wealth in their homes.

The bad news is that a smaller share of these new homeowners is stretched thin, vulnerable to the least shock, saving very little, with high levels of consumer debt, at the mercy of predatory lenders, being forced to sell their houses early, and often ending up in foreclosure.

Chapter 4 examines actual data on new house purchases, new mortgages, foreclosures, and wealth creation to see how these gains and losses have been distributed and are likely to be distributed in the future.

If the new homeowners had not become that, of course, they would have rented. Hence it is important to examine rental markets along with ownership markets, to make sure that these new homeowners are attracted into homeowning, not pushed in by the absence of available rental properties.

Unfortunately, conditions in the rental market are not very good either. Many renters have low and moderate incomes, and wages in these income levels declined in the 1980s, leading to the so-called hollowing out of the income distribution. Yet the nation has gone through an overall housing boom where prices have risen sharply, much more so than incomes for low- and moderate-income households.

The combination has put the squeeze on low- and moderate-income households, whether they own or rent. According to tabulations by the Joint Center for Housing Studies using data from the American Community Surveys, very large shares of low-income households—45 percent among owners and 57 percent among renters—are spending more than half their disposable income on housing, the normal definition of households with serious affordability issues. Another 21 percent faces moderate cost burdens, spending between 30 and 50 percent of their disposable income on housing.[7] With spending at this level, households have very little left over for other needs. They are also likely to spend enormous amounts of time commuting to their jobs and away from their families.

On the supply side of the market, many properties have been removed from the available rental stock. There are numerous federal rent subsidy programs, but their effectiveness has been called into question, and expenditures have leveled off. A number of state and local policies also operate, perhaps unintentionally, to constrict the supply of affordable rental housing. The overall situation is not promising, especially if millions of foreclosed homes are taken out of supply (at least temporarily) and these homeowners are pushed back into an already-inadequate supply of rental housing.

Chapter 3, devoted to rental housing, will analyze the issues. It will review the overall rental situation, outline the criticisms of present programs, and suggest some new strategies. One obvious strategy involves plain-old expansion of supply. This may in turn involve more spending or a change in the mix of general income support and in-kind assistance. It will be extremely important to rethink the balance of responsibilities between the federal and state and local governments.

Chapter 3 also considers some promising new approaches for introducing ownership possibilities. The Department of Housing and Urban Development (HUD) has some experimental approaches for converting rent subsidies into down payment-escrow accounts. While at this point small numbers of potential homeowners have taken advantage of these possibilities, the particular experiences of these homeowners have been very favorable, with very low foreclosure rates (Lubell 2006). Unlike the open subprime mortgage market described earlier, most graduates of rent subsidy programs have undergone extensive homeowner counseling, and they may be more ready to take the step to ownership.

Of more quantitative importance is a new interest in manufactured housing, factory-built structures that can be located either on land owned by the homeowner or on land owned by an investor. In the former case, manufactured housing comes very close to normal single-family housing; in the latter case, it is a hybrid situation where the homeowner owns the structure and the landlord owns the land. Either way, manufactured housing is clearly cheaper than site-built housing. It is starting to make a real quantitative impact in many rural areas, particularly in the south. On the lending side, however, the results in the manufactured housing sector are essentially the same as in the rest of the subprime market, with low down payments and high foreclosures (Apgar et al. 2002).

The last issue to discuss is policy. It might be tempting to evaluate the subprime market, weighing the gains of homeowners who seem better off against the losses of those who seem worse off. But this type of assessment is not very meaningful. The opening up of mortgage markets happened, and at this point the changes are so fundamental that realistically they cannot be reversed. The nation cannot just close up the subprime mortgage market and go back to the ownership rates of a decade ago. Rather, the task is to manage the new situation and see if policy measures can retain the benefits of the new burst in ownership while lessening the costs.

Many types of policy changes might be considered. One set of potential changes affects the rental market. As argued above, significant expansions in supply could be considered, especially if house prices do not begin declining. Alterations in rent subsidy policies should be considered, in particular to give local authorities more power to tailor present subsidies to the needs of their own communities. There should also be new attention to rent-to-own possibilities and measures to improve the functioning of the manufactured housing market.

Another set of changes involves the mortgage market itself. Other product markets often have powerful incentives for suppliers to police themselves, and this self-policing could happen in the subprime market. Loans are often sold "with recourse," meaning that if there are problems in the lending process, the lender is liable to take back the loan. Such provisions have not been much used until recently, but they do give lenders a powerful incentive to keep the process clean.

At a broader level, the Mortgage Bankers Association has developed a set of "best practices," as have various state associations. These organizations could participate in grading institutions, loan products, or the like, or focus on making sure their members comply with the general guidelines.

Increased governmental regulation is another possibility. For high-cost mortgages, a federal statute—the Home Owner Equity Protection Act of 1994 (HOEPA)—provides some protections, preventing balloon payments (large scheduled increases in mortgage payments) in the first five years of a mortgage and prepayment penalties that last longer than five years. While the actual coverage of HOEPA loans is minimal, the statute's provisions seem to lead lenders, and it could be used to guide the market.

HOEPA coverage could be extended to more subprime loans, and HOEPA could be used to prevent or limit various practices that have caused problems, as the Federal Reserve has already done. One set of measures that might be particularly important would extend the balloon payment provision to payment shocks more broadly, including the APR or monthly payments implicit in ARMs. With such changes, lenders might not be so ready to offer teasers or souped-up ARMs if they could not easily raise their mortgage payments back up. The HOEPA structure could also be used to make it much more costly for lenders to offer ARMs than fixed-rate mortgages.

Lenders and brokers in the subprime market should also face tighter supervision. Many lenders in the subprime market are either affiliates of banks and thrifts or their holding companies, not uniformly subject to direct supervision of their lending practices. Many independent mortgage companies are state-chartered and subject to even less scrutiny. Mortgage brokers are not really supervised at all. There were many abuses in this sector of the market, and there should be stronger efforts to police it. These measures are likely to require congressional legislation.

Large government-sponsored enterprises such as Fannie Mae and Freddie Mac play a huge role in mortgage markets generally, less so in the subprime market. But these enormous firms could step up their buying of subprime mortgages, or use their clout in other ways, to standardize and improve conditions in the subprime market, as they have done in the prime market. The Federal Housing Administration (FHA) and the Veterans Administration (VA) have been guaranteeing low-income mortgages for years. These mortgages are mainly long-term with fixed rates, not the instrument of choice in the new subprime market. FHA and VA might become more important, and stabilizing, factors once again by refinancing ARMs into long-term, fixed-rate mortgages.

The foreclosure process is governed by local laws, and local action is important too. By now there are many successful local anti-foreclosure programs, perhaps the most successful being the Home Ownership Protection Initiative (HOPI) in Chicago. The CBOs were helpful in getting HOPI going, they have gotten other initiatives going, and they are beginning to play a very active role in the fight against predatory lending and foreclosures more generally (Neighborhood Housing Services of Chicago 2006).

Indeed, in some respects the CBOs may be a secret weapon to improve the workings of the subprime market. Until now, CBOs have focused for the most part on expanding credit and homeownership. Now it may be time for CBOs to play defense and try to keep people in their homes. Anti-foreclosure efforts may be one aspect of this new fight, and promoting financial literacy may be another. Virtually every expert says that predatory lending and foreclosure problems would not be nearly as serious if borrowers were more literate financially.

Chapter 5, on potential policy changes, will examine all these issues.

2

The Evolution of This Market

Before World War II, mortgage credit markets played a limited role in American life. Most households who bought houses were upper income, relying largely on their accumulated savings. Banks were the main lenders then, but many banks were not very healthy, having suffered serious losses (and often outright failures) in the Great Depression. Deposit insurance was a very new item at the time.

That all changed at the close of the war, with the development of the prime mortgage market. The Depression and high unemployment of the 1930s were over, and many families could look forward to rising income streams. Plus, many families came out of the war with huge forced savings that could be used for down payments. Innovative lenders took advantage of the situation and developed the now-classic 30-year, fixed-rate mortgage. This instrument permitted millions of middle-class homeowners to buy their homes, often in the suburbs, and it sparked America's first boom in homeownership.

By today's standards, the mortgage market of this postwar period looks pretty simple. The main holders of conventional single-family mortgages were institutions then called savings and loans, now called thrifts. These institutions were under the Federal Reserve's Regulation Q, which limited the deposit rates they could pay. This in turn limited the deposits institutions could raise to finance new mortgages. The institutions also had limits on their balance sheets that forced them to

13

buy mainly mortgages. They took in deposits and loaned the money back in the form of home-secured mortgages, usually long-term, fixed-rate mortgages.

Banks were also permitted to make conventional single-family mortgages, though not required to. But banks were also under the Federal Reserve's Regulation Q ceiling, which also limited the deposits banks could raise. Despite Regulation Q, the stock of mortgage debt outstanding under these conventional single-family mortgages grew from $40 billion in 1949 to $132 billion in 1960, an annual growth rate of 11 percent.[1] Logistically, borrowers desiring a mortgage would simply go to their friendly neighborhood thrift or bank and complete the paperwork.

The federal government played an important role in this early development of mortgage markets. In the 1930s and 1940s, the government set up the Federal Housing Administration and the Veterans Administration to guarantee mortgages to lower-income households, and the Federal National Mortgage Corporation (now called Fannie Mae) to purchase and sell FHA and VA loans. The Federal Home Loan Banks (FHLBs) were established to provide funding for thrift institutions.

Aggregate government-insured mortgages from the FHA and VA amounted to about half as much as private conventional mortgages in 1949, with an outstanding mortgage debt stock of $15 billion. These mortgages too grew in the 1950s, to $56 billion by 1960.[2]

Beginning in the 1960s, almost every aspect of this plain-vanilla mortgage market of the 1950s underwent significant changes. In the 1960s the thrift institutions were buffeted by what was known as the "disintermediation" crisis. Market interest rates rose, partly because inflation was then accelerating and an inflation premium was tacked onto market interest rates. Depositors could get a better return on their money by investing directly in market securities, like Treasury bills, than in the Regulation-Q-capped deposits of thrifts and banks. Depositors began to pull their funds from the thrifts and banks, leaving the thrifts in a very precarious position. Thrifts had to invest in mortgages, they had no new funds coming in to make new high-rate investments, and they were stuck with the long-term low-rate mortgages from earlier years. Their immediate financial crisis was ameliorated by funding from the FHLBs and later by the elimination of Regulation Q ceilings. These changes permitted thrifts to pay a higher rate on deposits, get new funds, and make higher-rate mortgages. But thrifts were still suffering losses on their earlier mortgages. Still later, their balance sheet restrictions were eliminated and they were allowed to operate across state borders. The constraints on the FHLBs were relaxed as well, and these banks now look much like normal commercial banks.

But many thrifts remained in a precarious financial position. That problem was compounded when some thrifts began to gamble to attract more deposits by paying high interest rates. Even more recently, other thrifts began to feel they could compete only if they too increased their interest rates to riskier levels. When these interest rates on short-term deposits became too high relative to the rates on their portfolios (composed mainly of fixed-rate mortgages), many thrifts began to fail, and the highly publicized saving and loan financial crisis of the 1980s arose. In the end, it cost taxpayers more than $100 billion to bail out failed thrifts.

The bank, too, suffered as a result of disintermediation. Regulation Q ceilings and the prohibitions against interstate banking were lifted for banks as well. But banks had never invested as heavily in long-term mortgages, so there were far fewer failed institutions, and the bailout costs were much smaller.

A second important development involved the growth in the secondary market for mortgages. In 1968, Fannie Mae's charter was altered to permit it to buy conventional mortgages, along with its earlier portfolio of government-insured mortgages. The Government National Mortgage Association (now called Ginnie Mae) was established to purchase FHA and VA mortgages. Two years later, the Federal Home Loan Mortgage Corporation (now called Freddie Mac) was created to bring more liquidity to the thrifts by buying their mortgages. All three of these secondary mortgage institutions, called government-sponsored enterprises (GSEs), provided new infusions of funds to the prime mortgage market, through the creation of a vigorous secondary mortgage market. This secondary market has now grown to huge proportions, with about 70 percent of new mortgages being sold onto the secondary market. It is now routine for direct lenders such as banks and thrifts to make mortgages and replenish their funds by selling the mortgages to the GSEs. The three GSEs now hold over $5 trillion of total mortgages.[3]

Fannie Mae and Freddie Mac have significantly affected the prime mortgage market in other ways. These GSEs hold some of their purchased mortgages on their own balance sheet, but they have also started the trend of securitizing mortgages and passing them onto the general capital market. They package these mortgages into bundles where risks are pooled. Fannie Mae and Freddie Mac manage the risks and relieve new investors of the burden of evaluating the risk of nonpayment mortgage by mortgage. These securities are then sold to direct investors, further broadening the funding sources for the prime mortgage market. The whole operation greatly enhances the pools of capital for the mortgage market while it diversifies and reduces risk. Simultaneously, the GSEs have used their leverage to standardize mortgage products, insure the mortgages, and perform underwriting functions.

A third important change was the disappearance of state usury law ceilings on mortgage rates. Through the 1960s and 1970s, many states imposed these usury law ceilings, which effectively cut low- and moderate-income borrowers out of mortgages markets. If these potential borrowers had incomes too low to qualify for prime credit, or checkered credit histories, lenders would simply deny credit. But the Depository Institutions Deregulatory and Monetary Control Act of 1980 prevented states from imposing usury law ceilings on first-lien mortgages, and many states followed the federal lead by removing all their ceilings on other mortgages. As a consequence, new borrowers who did not qualify for prime credit were able to get subprime credit, at higher interest rates. More than anything else, this elimination of usury law ceilings paved the way for the development of the subprime market.

There were other important changes. Borrowers unable to come up with the standard 20 percent down payment were able to get private mortgage insurance (PMI) to insure their liability. Recognizing the risk of losses on most foreclosures when down payments were low, lenders typically required PMI on most mortgages with loan-to-value ratios exceeding 80 percent. Later on, piggyback loans were developed, in which second-lien (second claim on the house) mortgages were piggybacked on first-lien mortgages. Lately the dollar volume of these piggyback mortgages has been growing rapidly, leading to a rising incidence of loans on which there is virtually no down payment.

In other credit markets, lenders for automobiles, credit cards, and other types of loans were simultaneously learning how to price credit differentially for borrowers with different probabilities of repayment. This process ultimately led to the development of credit scoring techniques and automatic processing of loan applications. The recent rise in mortgage borrowing saw the spread of these automatic underwriting techniques to the subprime mortgage market. By the early 2000s, some lenders were offering to process mortgage applications in less than 15 minutes.

The Subprime Mortgage Market

All these factors set the preconditions for today's open, but complicated, subprime mortgage market. While there are different definitions of exactly what is meant by a subprime mortgage loan, there is no doubt that there has been huge growth in the market, from almost nothing 10 years ago to something like 20 percent of total mortgage originations now (using the numbers shown in chapter 1). This total excludes parallel lending by the old-line government-insured lenders, FHA and VA. These agencies still guarantee loans to first-time borrowers who may not qualify for prime loans. In earlier years FHA and VA would have dominated the private subprime market, but now the subprime market has moved way past the FHA-VA market, which represented only 5 percent of first-lien mortgages in 2005 (Avery, Brevoort, and Canner 2006).

Subprime mortgage loans are basically loans to borrowers who do not qualify for prime mortgage loans. These loans carry higher interest rates than prime mortgages, generally on the order of 3 to 5 percentage points, and higher points and fees. When points and fees are amortized, the average percentage rate on subprime loans is often in double digits, perhaps 4 to 6 percentage points above the APR on prime mortgages of comparable maturity. This may sound like a bad deal, but since subprime mortgages are secured by the value of the house, just as in the prime market, the APR on subprime mortgages is still well below that on credit card borrowing. In this sense, the subprime market is still the cheapest source of credit for millions of potential borrowers.[4]

Whereas the standard prime mortgage is for 30 years at a fixed interest rate, the standard subprime mortgage is the 2/28—the mortgage rate is fixed for 2 years, and then becomes adjustable for 28. Or fixed for 3 years and then adjustable for 27 in a close cousin, the 3/27. This structure leads to two types of dangers. First, vulnerable and perhaps gullible borrowers can be tempted by teaser rates, low for two or three years but then much higher. Second, from a macroeconomic standpoint, short-term rates were unusually low in the past three years, but they have now reverted to more normal levels. Hence, even if lenders were not offering teasers, there could be a large payment shock in store for many subprime borrowers.

While the 2/28 (or 3/27) is the standard mortgage, subprime lenders offer a bewildering array of products, many of which feature easy terms up front. Common products are interest-only mortgages, which defer the payment of the principal of the loan for a number of years, payment-option adjustable rate mortgages that do not even force the borrower to pay all the interest, and the piggyback mortgages mentioned above, which combine first- and junior-lien loans. Beyond that, borrowers can have either documented or undocumented credit histories, documented or undocumented income and assets, low or no down payments, rates that are fixed or adjustable for almost any horizon, and so forth. If in the earlier period it was impossible for subprime borrowers to get credit, now these same borrowers are often swimming in a sea of possible loan products (Federal Reserve et al. 2006).

Economists studying the subprime mortgage market have noticed that low-down-payment requirements are correlated with higher default probabilities (Mason and Rosner 2007). Hence it is very natural that low-down-payment loans would carry higher interest rates to cover the higher default risks. Economists have also noticed a form of payment illusion. By law, the maximum rate on an ARM is stated in the loan document, but lenders are myopic when it comes to factoring in this maximum rate (Bucks and Pence 2006).

Subprime mortgages are much more likely than prime mortgages to contain prepayment penalties, fees that a borrower must pay to the lender to be able to repay the entire balance of the loan early. According to Fannie Mae estimates, 80 percent of subprime mortgages have prepayment penalties, while only 2 percent of prime mortgages do (Zigas, Parry, and Weech 2002). This makes it much more costly for borrowers to get out of subprime mortgages than prime mortgages. But as we will see, many subprime borrowers are still forced to refinance often, and they usually lose their pounds of flesh in prepayment penalties.

The elimination of usury ceilings has permitted lenders to price credit appropriately—they no longer have to deny borrowers with uncertain income or repayment prospects. As a consequence, mortgage denial rates, as reported under the Home Mortgage Disclosure Act (HMDA), have fallen over the period.

As in other credit markets, credit scores—essentially, grades on how well borrowers have met past obligations—have been highly developed. These credit scores now accurately predict defaults and delinquencies for other credit markets. Credit scores can be, and are, used relatively automatically by lenders to approve loans and to allocate borrowers to different types of loans—prime, subprime, and so on. The relative automaticity of the new process is desirable, as is the opening of the subprime window to new borrowers. Neither racial nor ethnic identities are recorded in credit scores, and mortgages are generally made without knowledge of the race or ethnicity of the borrower.

But there are some less attractive aspects. For one thing, the statistical relationships on which credit scoring depends are taken from other markets. The subprime mortgage market did not exist 10 years ago, and there are certainly no data on which to base credit scores for periods when interest rates are particularly low, house prices are behaving in unique ways, and so forth. In fact, this 10-year period largely coincided with fairly significant appreciation of house prices—far beyond what is normal relative to growth in the economy—providing a bit of security to both lender and borrower in the form of appreciating capital that could be tapped when other events, such as unemployment, occurred. The statistical foundations of credit scoring in the subprime mortgage market will need a cycle or two to establish relationships.

Further, in this new world it is complicated and confusing for borrowers to search out all their available options, to understand all the terms of the loans, and to avoid getting misallocated into a lower credit category than may be appropriate. In the end the process by which rates are set is regulated by the borrower's ability to shop around, and prospective borrowers may not know where to shop, what to ask, or how to evaluate their own credit-worthiness (Fishbein and Woodall 2006).

One institution that has sprung up in the new mortgage market is that of the independent mortgage broker. These mortgage brokers are agents who market mortgages and receive a commission on their successful transactions. Brokers have become pervasive and operate in virtually all communities, but they are especially plentiful in areas underserved by old-line commercial banks and thrifts, such as minority communities. They keep an open door, and have an incentive to make mortgage deals. There has been a huge rise in the number of independent mortgage brokers, from an estimated 7,000 firms in 1987 to an estimated 53,000 firms in 2004, the latest count available (Apgar and Fishbein 2005).[5] While many of these new brokers operate in the prime market, their importance is much greater in the subprime market. In 2005, about 60 percent of all subprime mortgages were placed through brokers, compared with 25 percent for the prime market (Apgar and Fishbein 2005).[6]

There is good and bad news in this growth of mortgage brokers. The prevalence of brokers has opened up the market and made it easier for prospective low- and moderate-income borrowers, and minorities, to find mortgages. But the brokers have minimal incentives to find the cheapest mortgage for borrowers, and only indirect incentives (through repeat business possibilities) to minimize repayment risks for lenders. Many contracts contain provisions called yield-spread premiums that borrowers effectively pay to brokers to permit brokers to cover their costs. But these yield-spread premiums are unregulated, and they can encourage brokers to steer borrowers into high-interest loans, with the brokers getting compensated by the borrowers for the increase in yield.

There are many indications that broker-originated loans are more likely to get into trouble than non-broker-originated loans. Delinquency and foreclosure rates are much higher in the subprime market, where brokers are much more prevalent. Survey evidence indicates that subprime brokers are not always very knowledgeable about the mortgage process and where their clients can get their best deal. Brokers are also much more likely to advertise and to search out and initiate contacts with prospective borrowers, rather than the other way around—a dangerous sign. And broker profits are high and apparently unrelated to the effort required to process the loan application, which is surely a very bad sign (Guttentag 2001).[7]

The subprime market is much less supervised than the prime market. In the prime market most mortgages are made by banks and thrifts, institutions that undergo rigorous bank examinations from their regulators—the Office of Controller of the Currency (OCC), the Office of Thrift Supervision (OTS), the Federal Deposit Insurance Corporation, and the Federal Reserve Board (the Fed). Table 2.1 lists the 10 largest prime market lenders, all of which are tightly supervised banks and thrifts.

These bank or thrift exams take place on a three-year cycle. Teams of examiners look at the lending records of the institution and the HMDA reports. Examiners also check for lending discrimination, which still seems to be a significant problem in the mortgage market, and the degree to which the lender evaluates the borrower's ability to make mortgage payments.

In the subprime market, the three largest subprime lenders in 2005 were independent mortgage companies, chartered by states and not subject to supervision by any bank or thrift regulators (see table 2.1). More complete tabulations from the 2005 HMDA data indicate that only 20 percent of

Table 2.1. Ten Largest Prime and Subprime Lenders, 2005

Institution	Type	Number of loans
Prime Lenders		
Countrywide Finance Company	Bank	825,429
Wells Fargo & Company	Bank	791,208
Washington Mutual Bank	Thrift	416,053
Bank of America	Bank	411,750
JP Morgan Chase	Bank	365,516
GMAC Bank	Thrift	314,264
National City Corporation	Bank	252,710
Wachovia Corporation	Bank	247,773
Citigroup	Bank	202,259
ABN AMRO	Bank	197,383
Subprime Lenders		
Ameriquest	Independent	342,937
H & R Block	Independent	192,230
New Century Mortgage Corp.	Independent	190,394
Countrywide Finance Company	Bank	190,205
HSBC Holding Company	Bank	186,860
National City Corporation	Bank	177,509
Fremont Investment and Loan	Thrift	172,781
Washington Mutual Bank	Thrift	161,137
Lehman Brothers Bank	Thrift	142,093
Wells Fargo & Company	Bank	130,588

Source: Home Mortgage Disclosure Act data.

subprime loans were made by supervised entities, with 29 percent made by more lightly supervised subsidiaries and affiliates of supervised lenders and a full 51 percent made by unsupervised mortgage companies. The subsidiaries of supervised lenders are usually supervised more lightly than their parent; the parents or holding companies supervise the lending activities of subsidiaries but do not directly supervise them.

But independent mortgage companies are just that, not supervised at all at the federal level. And, they finance themselves in capital markets, not through deposits. This forms a gigantic hole in the supervisory safety net, a topic covered in chapter 5.

The federal banking agencies recently posted an advisory notice against many suspect lending practices. This advisory went to banks and thrifts, and indirectly to their affiliates, but did not even cover the lenders that make over half the subprime loans. A number of states tried to close the gap by applying the federal advisory to all lenders in their state.

Nor are the many independent mortgage brokers federally supervised. Some states may regulate brokers or lenders, but the resources states devote to supervision are trivial compared with the federal government's. The Federal Trade Commission can adjudicate complaints after the fact, if abuses are widespread. But after-the-fact measures are far less comprehensive than the continuing supervision of prime market lenders.

Capital Markets

It is impossible to understand the behavior of the new subprime mortgage market without examining the influence of capital markets. As described above, these were brought into the prime mortgage market largely through the GSEs. But the GSEs do not play nearly as great a role in the subprime mortgage market as they do in the prime market. Many subprime mortgages do not qualify for the underwriting standards of Fannie Mae and Freddie Mac, and these GSEs do not purchase subprime loans nearly as automatically as they do prime mortgage loans. Moreover, while the GSEs led the way in prime market securitizations two decades ago, by now many large financial institutions have learned how the process works and have taken it to new levels.

These securitizations happen in much the same way as in the prime market. Large lenders or other financial intermediaries pool subprime loans, along with other loans, into securities that diversify risks. These securities are sold directly onto capital markets, and bought by large investors. Investors can in turn pass the securities onto hedge funds, to foreign investors, or to even further structured finance instruments called collateralized debt obligations. In the end the financial complexities are such that it is almost impossible to tell what investor is holding what share of what loan. Risks are calculated by computers and then spread to the winds.[8]

The advantage of this situation is that, as in the prime market (where similar developments have taken place), the introduction of capital markets greatly broadens the source of funds for borrowers and diversifies risks for lenders. The process is efficient, time-saving, and impersonal, with no obvious discrimination against certain classes of borrowers. If there is a collapse or a foreclosure, losses are likely borne in tiny part by many, many investors.

But debate rages about whether this dissipation of risks causes other problems. One argument is that since lenders just make loans and pass them on, there is little incentive for lenders to police the lending process and little incentive for buyers of mortgage-backed securities to guard against defects in the lending process. No single investor will take much loss, and no single investor should care about any deficiencies in the lending process. Risk diminution has allegedly led to buyer and lender carelessness.[9]

There is another side to the story. Lenders typically sell loans "with recourse," which means these lenders must take back loans if there are problems in the lending process. As long as foreclosures were low and lenders were optimistic, nobody seemed to worry much about recourse clauses, and some sales agreements even omitted them. But if loans start nonperforming almost immediately after they are made, and if foreclosures threaten to become a significant factor, potential buyers of loans will start to watch the recourse clauses, and they will force the lenders to take back the bad loans. Exactly this seems to be happening in the current cycle; news stories lately mention fancy lawyers hired by the Wall Street investors going up against small country bank lenders to get them to take back the soft loans.

This all suggests that there may be more incentive for lenders to be careful about their loans than is commonly imagined. In the go-go years of the early 2000s, recourse clauses may not have been much of a factor, but they are becoming a big factor in 2007. And they will likely be a factor from now on—even Wall Street firms do not like to lose money on subprime mortgages, however widely the losses are spread. Now that certain weaknesses in the subprime lending process have been exposed, everybody in the process will probably be much more careful. Lenders will document their processes better, and buyers and securitizers of loans will make sure this is done.

Government Regulation

While there is less supervision in the subprime market than the prime market, and while the subprime market has developed because of the elimination of usury ceilings and balance sheet constraints on lenders, a number of overarching federal regulations still pertain to the subprime market, and to the prime market for low- and moderate-income mortgages more generally. These regulations have played, and should continue to play, an important role in the functioning of the subprime market.

The most important focus of regulation has been racial discrimination. Racial minorities were basically shut out of the first American housing boom at the close of World War II. Real estate brokers would allegedly draw red lines around districts where lenders would refuse to make loans, giving rise to the term "redlining." In an attempt to combat this discrimination, the federal government passed both the Fair Housing Act of 1968 and the Equal Credit Opportunity Act of 1974. The Community Reinvestment Act of 1977 was also passed originally as an antidote to redlining.

But the statute that has become the most important in fighting housing and credit discrimination has turned out to be a disclosure statute, the Home Mortgage Disclosure Act of 1975. This act required lenders to report their mortgage loans by race, sex, and census tract. In 1989 the Federal Reserve, which administers the act, strengthened it to require the reporting of mortgage denial rates. Then, in 2004, when denial rates were becoming less meaningful because of the differential pricing of credit, the Fed strengthened the act once again to require reporting of the APR for high-priced loans, defined as mortgage loans with an APR three points above the Treasury rate for a security of the same maturity.

In 1989, at about the time of the initial recording of denial rates, the *Atlanta Journal Constitution* ran a series called "The Color of Money" that showed significant credit discrimination against minorities. This information was used by the Justice Department to bring an action against the Atlanta-based Decatur Federal Savings and Loan. Shortly thereafter, the Federal Reserve Bank of Boston enhanced the HMDA data with additional questions that also showed presumptive evidence of discrimination. The Boston Fed data have been much studied by economists.[10]

The question of exactly how important this discrimination is today is still under discussion. Some disparities in loan provisions can be justified by the fact that blacks have lower incomes than whites, fewer assets, and worse credit histories. Yet, housing and mortgage markets have become so complicated that discrimination seems to take place in many subtle ways—the making of loans, the provision of information, the steering of customers to prime and subprime markets, the showing of properties, and so forth. It has become very difficult to assess and police all these different avenues (Ross and Yinger 2002; Turner, Richardson, and Ross 2007; Turner et al. 2002).

In terms of the HMDA data, while overall mortgage denial rates have gone down, as lenders have resorted less to outright denial and more to differential pricing of credit, denial rates are still much higher for blacks than whites. For first-lien home purchase loans in 2005 these denial rates were 29 percent for blacks as opposed to 15 percent for non-Hispanic whites (see figure 1.3). The racial incidence of subprime lending showed even greater differentials, with 54.7 percent of mortgage loans to blacks being high-priced (essentially in the subprime market), compared with 17.2 percent for non-Hispanic whites (Avery et al. 2006).

Since blacks are worse credit risks due to lower incomes, one might expect them to face higher denial rates and a higher incidence of subprime loans. But the independent variables do not justify the enormous disparities shown in the HMDA data for today's loans. Many economists have fit regressions to try to explain the differentials, usually arriving at the verdict that some, but not all, disparities in denial rates and the incidence of subprime loans can be explained with normal quantitative independent variables. There still seems to be significant evidence of some discrimination in the credit process (Avery et al. 2006).

On the supervisory front, the regulators of banks and thrifts have the HMDA data lender by lender, and are going through them with an aim to bringing suits and fines whenever appropriate. Many lenders are now in the position of having to justify their lending disparities to their regulators, though reporters have pointed out an absence of publicized enforcements.

A second important regulatory constraint involves the Community Reinvestment Act. Initially passed as an antidote to redlining, the act has become a type of political trade for deposit insurance. Banks and thrifts benefit from deposit insurance, and as a trade-off, they are supposed to plow a certain share of their deposit funds back into low- and moderate-income mortgages in their communities. Banks and thrifts are also supposed to make small business and farm loans, to the extent these are relevant in the bank's regional sphere of business. This regional sphere is called the bank's assessment area. Every three years, along with its normal examination, the bank or thrift is graded on its CRA performance. Banks or thrifts can receive grades of outstanding (about 20 percent of the time), satisfactory (about 75 percent of the time), or needs improvement (about 5 percent of the time) (Gramlich 1999).

Only about one-third of CRA mortgage loans to low- and moderate-income households have rates high enough to be considered subprime.[11] Lending institutions are free to set the interest rate in the usual way, and the majority of borrowers, even those with low incomes, receive prime mortgage treatment. But the loans are all supposed to go to low- and moderate-income borrowers, measured by whether the borrower's income is less than 80 percent of the metropolitan-wide area median.

CRA has an unusual penalty structure. There is no explicit fine or reprimand for banks and thrifts that receive a CRA grade of "needs improvement." At the same time, the institution's CRA grades are made public, and banks and thrifts view a grade of "needs improvement" as a black mark. Indeed, many institutions view a "satisfactory" grade as a black mark. The Federal Reserve can hold up mergers when any of the banks or thrifts desiring to merge has a low CRA grade, but this happens rarely. The main incentive for banks and thrifts to avoid a bad CRA grade seems to be the unfavorable publicity.

CRA was strongly resisted when it was first passed back in 1977, but it has become much less controversial. Some banks still would like to get rid of the law, and some economists still criticize the law as a form of credit control—a coercive interference with the normal functioning of the free market (Benston 1997). At the same time, one can view CRA as a helpful push in the direction of opening up credit markets to low- and moderate-income borrowers. Before CRA banks and thrifts made very few of these loans, now they make more than $100 billion worth a year. The repayment experience has been very good on these loans, with delinquency and foreclosure rates rivaling those in the prime market for much higher-income borrowers (Board of Governors of the Federal Reserve System 2000).

Basically, CRA seems to have nudged banks and thrifts in the direction of making more low- and moderate-income mortgages, the banks and thrifts have done that, and they have found, perhaps to their great surprise, that this new lending is good business. Today you will find many fans of CRA, even among the institutions regulated by the law. And you will find more than $100 billion a year in mortgages to low- and moderate-income households, most with very reasonable interest rate and loan terms. A large share of these loans probably would not have been made without the law.

A third important regulation influencing the subprime market, and again the market for low- and moderate-income mortgages more generally, involves the housing goals set by the Department of Housing and Urban Development. These are goals that HUD places on Fannie Mae and Freddie Mac, the two big privatized secondary market mortgage purchasers. These HUD housing goals can be viewed as a political trade-off for some indirect benefits conferred to the GSEs. While Fannie Mae and Freddie Mac are technically private, listed on private stock exchanges and with private stockholders, and while their borrowing is for the most part not explicitly guaranteed by the federal government, the two agencies still have some borrowing privileges with the Treasury. Participants in credit markets still seem to believe that the Treasury would come to the aid of Fannie Mae or Freddie Mac if the purchaser were to have a liquidity or financial crisis. Hence even though there is no explicit government guarantee, Fannie Mae and Freddie Mac can borrow more cheaply in credit markets than other institutions of their size and risk (Passmore 2003).

As a political trade for this perception advantage, and for some other more technical privileges, HUD places housing goals, or performance constraints, on Fannie Mae and Freddie Mac. Until now these constraints have been in terms of market share: in 2005, for example, Fannie Mae and Freddie Mac were required to purchase 52 percent of total low- and moderate-income mortgage loans, 37 percent of mortgage loans in underserved areas, and 22 percent of some special affordable mortgage loans. Historically, when the overriding need was to increase low-income lending, these market-share goals might have made sense, but now the problems may be changing. Many types of mortgages are now available to low- and moderate-income borrowers, and leading thinkers feel that the main problem is enforcing sensible lending standards within the subprime market, rather than just promoting market shares. I return to this issue in chapter 5.

The enforcement mechanism for these housing goals is similar to that for CRA. As with CRA, Fannie Mae and Freddie Mac would definitely suffer bad publicity if they were not to fulfill their goals. In recent years, Congress has been almost continuously reviewing the accounting standards and charters of Fannie Mae and Freddie Mac—in particular, whether these charters should be rewritten to limit the activities and/or profits of the two lenders. Given these political constraints, Fannie Mae and Freddie Mac have not been willing to risk congressional disapproval, and they have stayed safely above their housing goals.

A fourth set of constraints involves very high cost mortgage loans, the high-cost portion of the subprime market. These high-cost loans fall under the Home Owner Equity Protection Act of 1994. The HOEPA approach is to shine a bright spotlight on high-cost subprime loans. For these loans, HOEPA bans balloon payments (large scheduled increases in mortgage payments) in the first five years and prepayment penalty periods that last longer than five years. HOEPA also enforces on lenders a practice of verifying the borrower's ability to repay the loan. The latter provision tries to insure that lenders are trying to make loans that can be repaid, not simply going after the asset value of the property in a foreclosure proceeding.

To prevent buyers of HOEPA loans from avoiding responsibility for any misinformation at the time of the loan, these buyers must take responsibility for actions of the lender, a provision known as assignee liability. This assignee liability provision makes it particularly difficult to sell HOEPA loans.

The Federal Reserve is given authority to adjust the HOEPA provisions within certain limits, and the Fed recently cut the thresholds defining high-cost loans to an APR of 8 percentage points above the Treasury rate on comparable securities. At the time, the Fed staff thought that the provision would bring about half of all subprime mortgage loans under HOEPA coverage. But lenders apparently modified their rates enough that, in the end, HOEPA covered only about 1 percent of subprime mortgage loans.[12]

HOEPA also has a points and fees test—loans with particularly high points and fees (about $500 today) are given HOEPA protection. The Fed is also empowered to determine what particular points and fees are to be included in the test, and it can discourage use of particular products by including their costs in the points and fees test. Recently, the Fed did just that for a product known as single premium credit insurance (SPCI). SPCI is financed in the initial mortgage (this is the single premium), meaning payments continue as long as the mortgage lasts, often long after the insurance itself has lapsed. Testimony indicated consistently that borrowers did not understand that SPCI was optional, and that it normally benefited them very little and cost them very much. High-pressure sales techniques often obscured these realities in the minds of poorly informed borrowers.

For a time, SPCI became the poster child of predatory lending, present in 28 percent of first-lien subprime mortgages and 48 percent of second-lien subprime mortgages, according to Fannie Mae (Zigas et al. 2002). But once the Fed included SPCI in the points and fees test, all loans with SPCI came under the HOEPA protections, greatly reducing the incentive for lenders to offer the product. Many prominent subprime lenders dropped the product altogether, selling their mortgage insurance instead on a pay-as-you-go basis, where borrowers could decide to renew it periodically. SPCI is now rarely used, at least one success story in the attempt to clean up the subprime market. This example shows how despite their limited coverage, the HOEPA provisions can be used to lead the whole subprime market.

At the latest count, about 40 states also try to regulate conditions in the subprime market using an approach similar to HOEPA's. Generally these state laws have tighter high-cost loan thresholds and more prohibitions against specific lending practices. Even though most states follow the general model of HOEPA, enough dimensions can be varied that state requirements differ significantly. National lenders complain about the "crazy quilt" of state regulation, and they often lobby to be relieved of state regulation. The OCC, which regulates national banks, invoked a Civil War statute to exempt, or preempt, its national banks from state regulation. The state regulators protested, but in 2007 the validity of OCC's preemption claim was confirmed by the Supreme Court. National banks will now be regulated by OCC. Other lenders without a national charter will stay under the purview of state law.

Beyond HOEPA, there are also standards for disclosure and for computing APRs under the Truth in Lending Act, standards for real estate settlement procedures under the Real Estate Settlements and Procedures Act (RESPA), and standards for accuracy in providing information for credit scores under the Fair Credit Reporting Act.

All these measures provide some federal ground rules in both the prime and subprime mortgage markets. The antidiscrimination statutes try to keep the market open for minorities on the same terms as for whites. CRA tries to induce banks and thrifts to make more low- and moderate-income mortgage loans. HUD's housing goals for Fannie Mae and Freddie Mac try to ensure an active secondary market for these low-income loans. HOEPA tries to police the very high cost segment of this market, and the other statutes regulate recording and disclosure practices.

In a sense, the subprime market came into existence because of the elimination of some federal regulations on lender interest rates and balance sheets. But it is a mistake to think of this market as totally, or even largely, unregulated. A comprehensive set of regulations has already been developed to protect consumers, and it could be extended. Ideas for doing that are given in chapter 5.

Community-Based Organizations

One unique aspect of both the subprime mortgage market and the portion of the prime market that serves low- and moderate-income households and minorities is the prevalence of community-based organizations.

These groups can be broadly defined as nonprofit providers of housing services, home-buyer counseling, and foreclosure protection. There are a great many such organizations—about 4,000 now engaged in housing programs of one sort or another—building more than a million units of housing a year. Most of these 4,000 CBOs are small and independent, but a number are large and organized into national networks (Apgar and Fishbein 2005).

The more traditional organizations are called community development corporations (CDCs). As their name suggests, these are local entities engaged in housing and community development activities, but they are not financial entities. More than 200 of the larger ones are network affiliates of NeighborWorks America (formerly The Neighborhood Reinvestment Corporation). NWA was founded 30 years ago with funds from an earlier HUD program. It receives federal funding of slightly more than $100 million a year, and it doles this money out to its affiliates. These affiliates are located in large cities, small cities, and, lately, even rural areas. The affiliates focus mainly on homeownership, though some concentrate exclusively on rental housing. They fix up dilapidated housing, find responsible low- and moderate-income owners, and arrange mortgage financing with financial institutions, which normally receive CRA credit from local banks and thrifts for the new mortgage loans. As properties are sold, the funds can be used to repeat the whole process. The affiliates have also been highly successful at raising money from other sources—foundations, partnerships, city grants, and the like. Given its name, NWA focuses primarily on particular neighborhoods, rather than fixing up homes randomly throughout the city (NeighborWorks America 2006).

All new homeowners are given extensive counseling before being allowed to buy their homes and are warned to come to the network at the first suspicion that the homeowners will not meet their required mortgage payments. In addition to this lending counseling, in recent years NWA has initiated broad foreclosure-prevention programs that have been extended to cover borrowers who were not initially NWA clients. Over the whole network, NWA mobilizes total housing assistance of roughly twenty times its initial federal funding.

The newer organizations are called community development financial institutions (CDFIs). These groups are chartered by the Treasury Department. To receive a charter, a CDFI has to be certified as a financing entity—essentially, having a certain portion of its assets committed to financing—along with having a community development mission. CDFIs include such entities as community development banks, credit unions, microenterprises, and community facilities loan funds, often bank-like activities. The CDFIs can also apply for and draw funds from the CDFI fund in the Treasury Department. The fund began in 1994 under the Clinton administration, though there was a precursor in the preceding Bush administration.

Many of the larger and more active CDFIs, including the two largest— the Local Initiatives Support Corporation and the Enterprise Fund— participate in an association of CDFIs called the Opportunity Finance Network. OFN provides capital and leadership to its network, shares information on best practices, and even rates its CDFIs for effectiveness. Like the CDCs, the CDFIs focus on housing, but many operate on a broader range of social and economic needs within particular development areas— business development, social programs, and even day care centers and charter schools (Opportunity Finance Network 2006).

The CDFI funding model is different as well. Since CDFIs are financial entities, they finance many of their operations through bank-like operations and privately raised capital, though they also receive funding from governmental and foundation sources.

In addition to the CDCs and CDFIs tied to national networks, a large number of CBOs, indeed the vast majority, work independently. They raise money from private or local government sources and use the money to conduct either ownership or rental programs.

The biggest continuing problem for the CBOs, whatever their institutional form, is raising capital. Many CBOs, particularly CDFIs, have been, and continue to be, ingenious in funding themselves. Traditionally they have raised donations from foundations and other philanthropic sources, and they often qualify for public housing funds. Beyond that, they are now raising CRA funds from banks and using all these sources to raise capital by floating debt. Some advanced thinkers are even devising ways of securitizing their debt, much like mortgage debt is already securitized.

The financial and technical revolution that has changed the character of mortgage markets is affecting how CBOs operate in other ways. Historically the CBOs helped banks and other lenders find good borrowers, but this role has been largely supplanted by the automated data systems that lenders now use to screen borrowers and arrange mortgages. There also used to be highly publicized CRA agreements between lenders and CBOs, but the recent enforcement of CRA by the regulatory agencies has tended to focus more on actual lending data and less on publicized agreements.

And, as the banking sector has become more consolidated, it has become harder for CBOs to work with their friendly local bank, now much more likely to be a branch of a huge national or international financial corporation. Finally, with the growing acceptance of CRA, there may be less need for CBOs to play an advocacy role.

While the historical role of CBOs may be changing, the CBOs still perform many valuable functions. One such function is avoiding foreclosures. One clear antidote to foreclosure is providing alternative sources of capital for borrowers, including those who fall behind on their mortgage payments. For example, the OFN is creating a mortgage program that provides full funding of mortgages for low- and moderate-income households at long-term fixed rates, contains an automatic tie-in to Fannie Mae and other sources of secondary market capital, centralizes lending processes, and provides counseling. The idea is to establish a full-service subprime lender that enforces clean lending standards and can compete with other subprime lenders in providing credit to new borrowers. At latest word, the Bank of America was considering a similar program, an ironic example of the CBO portion of the market leading giant private entities.

Many effective local foreclosure-prevention programs are also initiated by CBOs. Other CBOs are learning how to tailor programs to the needs of their local communities. In addition, CBOs are adapting to the automatic underwriting and mortgage approval process, helping their clients navigate the modern credit world and being prepared to intervene in case of disputes or errors.

CBOs have always played, and should continue to play, an important role in homeowner counseling, often financed by foundations or bank CRA grants. With the complexity of modern credit markets, insuring consumer financial literacy has become a huge issue. CBOs are finding a ready toehold in this area, helping potential borrowers understand their options, how different mortgages work, and the likely costs and benefits of alternative means of financing. Often what appears as a problem in financial literacy is not that at all—borrowers are so desperate for funds, they will take any deal that entails up-front funding. In these cases, the CBOs will explain the benefits and costs, but they will often be able to tap into alternative sources of funds to prevent borrowers from getting locked into disadvantageous contracts. CBOs often partner with banks or other lenders in this area as well, relying on a provision that gives banks CRA credit for financial literacy programs.

Delinquencies, Foreclosures, and Predatory Lending

Surely the biggest problem with the subprime mortgage market, even before the latest collapse, is the heavy incidence of foreclosures. The wealth building that follows homeownership is great, but if low- and moderate-income households get foreclosed on their loans, these households typically lose all the equity they have accumulated in their homes. In these cases, the wealth building that is supposed to follow homeownership becomes wealth destruction.

Given the often-checkered histories of subprime borrowers, it would be natural to expect delinquency and foreclosure rates to be well above those in the prime market. And indeed they are well above, about ten times as high as in the prime market already and probably set to rise further, given the recent slackening of house price increases and the recent rise in short-term interest rates (Joint Center for Housing Studies 2006, figure 25). Other borrowers not actually in foreclosure are still delinquent on their loan payments, making these borrowers vulnerable to foreclosure pressure (Schloemer et al. 2006). Finally, foreclosures can be highly concentrated in particular urban areas.

As if this situation were not bad enough, things are complicated by the apparent presence of some new actors in the drama, predatory lenders. Obviously no lenders are explicitly labeled as predatory, and it is a bit of an art form to know exactly when a loan contract is predatory and when it is not. But the term has nevertheless been coined in recent years to describe the phenomenon of sharp lenders taking advantage of defenseless or financially illiterate borrowers. These lenders typically have much more knowledge of the types of products available and their benefits and costs to borrowers—an *information asymmetry,* in the language of economists. Often these lenders have loan quotas to meet, regardless of whether the loans would do the borrowers any good, and their salespeople use high-pressure techniques to meet their quotas. These salespeople are alleged to drive around neighborhoods, spot homes where it looks like borrowers will be needing credit, and take it from there. SPCI, now effectively stopped, was a common device by which predatory lenders took advantage of borrowers, as was asset-based lending, loan-flipping, and equity-stripping. There are also many reports of out-and-out fraud and abuse (Renuart 2004; Goldstein 2007).

Predatory lending is often mentioned in the same breath as the foreclosure problem, but these two phenomena are distinctly different. While predatory lending can certainly lead to foreclosure and while it has certainly been behind a great many foreclosures, not all foreclosures are due to predatory lending. Sometimes the loan process can be as clean as a whistle, with the borrower fully understanding all provisions of the loan and not operating under a competitive disadvantage. But the borrower can still get into trouble because of an insufficient financial cushion, a large payment shock, or a negative turn in income or health status.

The Federal Reserve's attempt to use the HOEPA provisions aggressively was one way to limit predatory lending, and the foreclosure problem more generally, through national policy. The OFN mortgage platform mentioned above is also a national program, this time organized privately. Many states have jumped into the fray with their own borrower-protection statutes, often modeled after HOEPA but with tighter provisions.

But since the actual foreclosure process is governed by local laws, it also makes sense to take local action against foreclosures. Under the prodding of many CBOs, this is now beginning to happen in many jurisdictions throughout the country, with encouraging success. One pathbreaker in this area has been a community group called Neighborhood Housing Service of Chicago (CNHS).

Between 1993 and 2002, the number of foreclosures in Chicago jumped 91 percent, from 4,923 to 9,431. These foreclosures were highly concentrated in particular areas. In three-quarters of the neighborhoods served by CNHS, the foreclosure rate was above 10 percent (Neighborhood Housing Services of Chicago 2006).

Foreclosures are very costly to many groups. At least temporarily, scarce supplies of low-income housing are taken out of service. Borrowers can lose most or all of the equity they have accumulated in their house. Many lenders maintain that even they do not benefit much from foreclosures—they lose an income-yielding mortgage, and they have large processing expenses. The Chicago City Government was also finding foreclosures very costly, particularly when it had to maintain and guard vacated structures. And, a high incidence of foreclosures is very bad for the neighborhood and for the property values of adjacent homes. Given all these interests, there is a clear logic in joint action to fight foreclosures.

CNHS became alarmed about the foreclosure problem. It partnered with the City of Chicago and the Federal Reserve Bank of Chicago, and the groups applied for funding from NWA. By 2003, the three groups had organized the Home Ownership Preservation Initiative. In the first two years of its operation HOPI saved 1,300 homes from foreclosure, dropping the overall foreclosure rate by 13 percent each year. HOPI also educated 4,000 Chicago households about the dangers of, and ways to combat, foreclosure (Neighborhood Housing Services of Chicago 2006).

The CNHS experience is encouraging because CNHS saw a problem, organized its resources, and achieved resounding successes. It partnered with other groups, such as the City of Chicago, that could also benefit if foreclosures were reduced. CNHS had a hot line and encouraged borrowers on the verge of missing payments to call in—it was much easier to work something out if the borrower was not already in foreclosure proceedings. Sometimes CNHS was able to arrange a loan-workout program, sometimes it was able to arrange a new source of credit, and sometimes it was able to sell the property and pay off the loan. The best general approach is for the borrower on the verge of delinquency to get in and see a counselor early, and the best approach for the CBO is to have lots of competent counselors ready to go early.

Conclusion

The chapter shows how the subprime mortgage market evolved from the conventional mortgage market of the 1950s. Despite its many problems, the new-style subprime mortgage market gives many additional households a chance at owning a home, something these households did not have in the 1950s. At the same time, the newer homeowners have much greater burdens placed on them than did the new homeowners of the 1950s. It is now much more complicated to shop for mortgages and find the best deal. It is also more likely families will face foreclosure, and it is easier for families to get taken advantage of. Chapter 4 will show how this new opening up of housing and mortgage markets has in fact worked out so far for the new homeowners.

3
Rental Housing

J ust as the market collapse of some subprime lenders cannot be understood without the fuller story of the market for homeownership, so the
market for homeownership cannot be understood without a more complete story about its alternative—renting. As mentioned earlier, most
low- and moderate-income households did not participate in the earlier
American boom in homeownership: they either preferred to rent or could
not meet the down payment or monthly payments necessary to qualify
for a mortgage. Most racial minorities did not participate because of discrimination, added to these other factors. All these families were in rental
housing.

Even with the recent surge in homeownership, the demand for rental
housing remains strong—for the young, the mobile, some minorities,
recent immigrants, the recently divorced or separated, and the relocated.
In addition, some groups with special needs—the potentially homeless, the
disabled, some elderly people—will always aspire to rental housing. About
a third of American households (34 million) have a more or less continuing demand for rental housing, and this demand has remained steady even
with the recent upward boost in homeownership rates.

For these reasons, conditions in the rental housing market form a significant backdrop to conditions in the ownership market. It is important
that the rental housing sector be strong and viable, with lots of options for
households making their choices. It is equally important to make sure that

households get pulled into homeownership because of its attractiveness, not pushed in by an absence of rental housing possibilities.

Federal policy has been important in the development and evolution of both ownership and rental markets. In the ownership market, federal policy changes have typically been enablers: FHA mortgages were the first guaranteed mortgages, Fannie Mae and Freddie Mac developed the secondary market and securitization, households were allowed to deduct interest and property taxes on their income tax returns, CRA stimulated low-income mortgages, and the fair housing laws set the underlying ground rules. But the subprime market developed more or less on its own, credit scoring developed on its own, and the prevalence of mortgage brokers was essentially a private phenomenon.

In the rental market, federal rent-support programs have played an important role ever since the 1930s. But these programs have always been small compared with the large private rental market and the federal tax subsidies given to homeownership.

Rent-Support Programs

Federal rent-support programs began in the 1930s, at about the same time as the initiation of the FHA. The Public Housing Act of 1937 initiated programs to build low-rent public housing facilities, turning these over to local public housing authorities to manage. For more than two decades, these supply-side programs were the federal government's answer to the problems of rental housing. They were controversial even then, as illustrated by widespread complaints in the 1950s about the "federal bulldozer" that razed neighborhoods to put up gigantic public housing structures.

The first expansion of this approach came in 1959 with Section 202 of the Housing Act. This provision authorized federal support for nonprofit corporations to operate cooperative rental housing for a population with special needs, the elderly and handicapped. Small-scale support programs for populations with special needs have been a staple of the federal approach ever since.[1]

The federal approach was broadened further in 1961 by Section 221.d.3 of the Housing Act, which authorized shallow interest-rate subsidies to nonprofit developers of low- and moderate-income rental facilities, with the facilities free to be converted to other uses after 20 years. In 1968,

Section 236 went even further by giving deeper interest-rate subsidies to private, for-profit developers of low- to moderate-income rental housing, again permitting conversions after 20 years.

The first rental housing assistance on the demand side of the market came in 1974, with the Section 8 program. Section 8 contained some supply-side subsidies for construction and rehabilitation of rental housing structures, but it also introduced subsidies that would be given on behalf of tenants, though to the owners of projects. The tenants could search for properties and choose among those meeting a set of physical standards, and their landlords were given the difference between the fair-market rent on these properties and 30 percent of the tenant's income. (From the beginning most federal programs have been structured so tenants do not pay more than 30 percent of their income in rent.)

In the early 1980s, most rental housing experts became much more interested in demand-side subsidies. Two housing experiments begun in the 1970s found that demand-side subsidies, or vouchers, stimulated very little increase in rents and were preferable on other grounds. The President's Commission on Housing of 1982 took a very strong interest in demand-side subsidies, as did many other groups (Apgar 1990). Perhaps because of this support, which came from both conservative and liberal analysts, the initial demand-side assistance of Section 8 was eventually transformed into a more flexible voucher program in 1987, and into one with portable vouchers in the Housing Choice Voucher Program of 1998. But the transition was not easy. The efficiency and equity arguments accepted by the Reagan administration accompanied proposals to reduce the size of many domestic programs, including housing subsidies. This led to opposition both by those fighting the Reagan Revolution and those providers and advocates who simply found it more comfortable to live within the status quo.

Even though federal expenditure programs gradually shifted in the direction of demand-side assistance, supply-side assistance programs were not abandoned. On the spending side, the HOPE VI program was created to target some of the most severely depressed public housing, including the earlier federal bulldozer programs. It permitted the wholesale redevelopment of large public housing structures, sometimes tearing them down, to promote better-planned community-wide development of housing facilities.

On the tax side, the Tax Reform Act of 1986 introduced the low-income housing tax credit (LIHTC). This tax credit program was deliberately

designed to compensate for the removal or reduction of other tax subsidies considered less efficient, less transparent, and less likely to accrue
to the benefit of the low-income renters themselves (e.g., tax-exempt
bonds that significantly benefited high-income taxpayers even if they
were used to promote rental housing). The LIHTC permits states to issue
sellable federal tax credits to private investors who agree to maintain
affordable rental units for 15 years, with the credits allotted to and administered by states. Recently, the LIHTC has been growing faster than programs like the Section 8 voucher program—implying a movement back
toward supply-side subsidies.

Other assistance programs work through state and local governments.
The Community Development Block Grant (CDBG), begun initially in
the Nixon administration, gives unconstrained general support to states
for community development activities. The HOME Investment Part-
nerships, authorized in 1990, provide additional funds for a wide range
of activities that include supply-side subsidies, demand subsidies, and
even some support for low-income homeowners.

Table 3.1 summarizes the federal spending programs that now benefit
housing and community development, in terms of outlays for 2005. Total
spending is $35 billion, of which block grants to state and local govern-
ments account for $7.4 billion; tenant-based rental assistance, $10 billion;
supply subsidies, $15.1 billion; and special needs housing programs for
the homeless, elderly, and disabled, $2.5 billion. None of these spending
programs has grown much in recent years.

Table 3.2 shows federal tax expenditures for housing, again for 2005.
The $3.9 billion for the LIHTC may seem like a large amount, but it
is dwarfed by tax expenditures for the mortgage interest deduction
($62.1 billion), the property tax deduction ($19.1 billion), the exclusion
of capital gains on houses from tax ($36.0 billion), and the exclusion of net
imputed rental income ($28.6 billion). Although many people associate
tax expenditures with mortgage interest deductions, homeowners also
benefit when they have equity in a home, since if they converted that equity
into a savings account, the interest on those savings would be taxed. All
these large tax expenditures mainly benefit high-income homeowners who
itemize deductions and pay high enough income taxes that the capital
gains exclusion generates real money.

The imbalance between relatively modest rent subsidy payments and
huge tax expenditures for high-income owners of real estate has generated
much comment. Housing advocates have used the contrast to argue for

Table 3.1. Federal Spending for Housing Programs, 2005 (billions of dollars)

Item	Expenditures
Block Grants	7.4
Community Development	5.0
HOME Investment Partnerships	1.7
Native American Housing	0.7
Tenant-Based Rental Assistance	10.0
Supply Subsidies	15.1
Public Housing Operating Fund	3.6
HOPE VI	0.7
Project-Based Rental Assistance	0.3
Public Housing Capital Fund	3.2
Housing Certificate Fund	7.3
Special Needs	2.5
Homeless	1.3
AIDS patients	0.3
Disabled	0.3
Elderly	0.9
Total	35.0

Source: Office of Management and Budget (2006b).

Table 3.2. Federal Tax Expenditures for Housing, 2005 (billions of dollars)

Item	Amount
Mortgage interest deduction	62.1
Property tax deduction	19.1
Exclusion of capital gains	36.0
Accelerated depreciation of rental housing	9.6
Low-income housing tax credit	3.9
Exclusion of net imputed rental income[a]	28.6
Other	8.9
Total	168.2

Source: Office of Management and Budget (2006a), table 19-1.

a. Net imputed rental income is gross imputed rental income (which is what is excluded from taxation for homeowners, less expenses such as mortgage interest and property tax). For instance, home-owners who have no mortgage and owe no property tax are also favored relative to those who would convert their equity in a home into a bank account on which interest income is taxable.

more low-income rent subsidy–type expenditures. Adam Carasso, Elizabeth Bell, Edgar Olsen, and Eugene Steuerle use the imbalance to draw what they call a U-shaped subsidy curve for housing (Carasso et al. 2005). Low-income households get some subsidies in the form of rent assistance, middle-income households get little, and high-income households get a lot. The point is clear, but the authors' alphabetic analysis is debatable. In reality, the curve looks more like a J, where low- and moderate-income subsidies are dwarfed by the tax subsidies to high-income homeowners.

This thumbnail sketch of the history of federal rental programs illustrates several other points. For one thing, there has not been a uniform strategy regarding how support should be conferred. The early programs were direct expenditures on the supply side, later morphing into some direct expenditures on the demand side, now supplemented by tax expenditures and other grants on the supply side. Often, particular projects had different sources of support layered on top of each other. Any of several approaches have intrinsic advantages and disadvantages, but there has never seemed to be a consistent policy strategy. The same is true of the respective role of the federal government and states and localities. Some programs have been federally financed and state-administered, some have been simply federal, and some have been federal grants to the states, with no consistent pattern.

Beyond this, there has been an underlying confusion of the goals of rental housing programs: are the programs simply for income support or do they have broader aims such as community enrichment or encouraging self-sufficiency? Should the programs be married to other social services or not? Are the programs trying to guide location, within or across urban areas, or are they intended to be neutral about location?

Partly because of the confusion of goals, and because the typical evaluations of the programs suggested that they were not achieving many if any of the possible goals, there has been intense criticism and discussion of federal rental assistance programs. Many programs have undergone periodic moratoria, hold-downs, and programmatic impasses while policymakers tried to hammer out new approaches. These days, many housing experts are calling for fairly major transformations of federal assistance programs.

The reexaminations are taking place in an era of substantial problems for rental housing. In the 1980s, low wages fell fairly dramatically relative to other wages, and in the 1990s, house prices went up more rapidly than other prices. The combination raised the relative price of affordable housing and put many low-income households in a bind, whether they owned or rented. Over 15 million households, 14 percent of the total, are now severely cost burdened, paying over half their income for housing costs, and another 19 million face moderate cost burdens, paying between 30 and 50 percent of their income. Problems are particularly serious in the lowest quintile of the income distribution, with more than half of all households facing severe cost burdens. As mentioned earlier, the burden rates are slightly higher for renters than owners: in the bottom income quintile, 57 percent of renters report serious burden, compared with 45 percent of owners.[2]

These basic economic facts are exacerbated by trends in the supply of rental properties. The nation has been losing affordable rental housing stock for almost three decades. Most affordable rental properties are not making money these days, and there has been a long-term trend toward converting these units to other purposes (Joint Center for Housing Studies 2006). The bubble in real estate values hit the homeownership market more than the rental housing market, and many rental housing owners found it much more profitable to convert units into condominiums, especially in areas where appreciation was the greatest and land scarcest. Many local areas already have a rental housing supply problem, and it could get worse. Local conditions also vary widely, with intense shortages of available rental housing in some areas and reasonable supplies in others.

Finally, there is a location dimension to the issue. Housing, whether rental or not, must be located somewhere, and that somewhere may not be ideal for its residents. Within urban metropolitan areas, available stocks of affordable rental housing are often located in bad neighborhoods, either crime-ridden or with inferior public schools, and often without reasonable access to jobs. In suburban areas where labor demand is growing, zoning restrictions and other regulations often prevent the development of affordable rental housing anywhere near these jobs. As a consequence, increasing numbers of low-income renters are being forced to commute long distances to work and to spend enormous amounts of time away from their families.

The partial collapse of the subprime market, and the increase in foreclosures, is likely to lead lenders—prime or subprime—toward more rigid requirements for making loans. In effect, an increased demand by renters for rental units may well be forthcoming at a time when that market already abounds with problems. It seems time for yet another reassessment.

The Design of Rental Assistance Programs

Rental assistance programs have often been discussed technically: the x program has y defects, and it might be modified in the z way. Such discussions often get bogged down in the complicated technical details of how to alter programs, and they lose sight of some of the broader issues. This chapter takes a different, and less detail-oriented, approach. It assesses from a theoretical standpoint how a nation might design its rental assistance programs anew. Actual suggestions for changing policies come up at the end of the assessment. The next four sections discuss design principles from the standpoint of particular or general support, demand or supply assistance, on the tax side of the budget or the spending side, and at the federal or state and local levels.

Income versus In-Kind Subsidies

Support for low-income renters can be given either as general income support or as in-kind assistance tied to housing. With general income support, households are in principle free to spend the support on anything; with in-kind support, household expenditures are tied to a particular form of expenditure, rental housing.

Economists generally prefer the income support approach for three reasons. The first is consumer choice. With a necessity good like housing, there may not be much difference—families have to spend a certain amount on housing. But assume that a family can make do with a slightly lower expenditure on housing than the support level for which it qualifies, devoting the extra money, say, to child care. Should it be free to do that, or forced to spend the entire amount on housing? With general income support, the family is free to do that; with a comparable amount of in-kind support, say housing vouchers, the family is not. If the in-kind subsidy is "thin," so the family is very unlikely to spend less than the subsidy on housing, there may be little difference on this dimension, but for large in-kind subsidies, there could be a major difference.

A second reason for preferring general income support is horizontal equity—treating families with equal needs equally. Present rental housing programs do not do this. Spaces are scarce in subsidized rental housing structures. Some eligible households get in and others do not, often on a first-come, first-served basis unrelated to the underlying needs of the family. Once a family gets in, it can stay, even if its income jumps a certain amount. This leads to a scattershot system of subsidies, where only about 33 percent of the lowest income renters, and only 40 percent of the lowest income elderly renters, receive any federal rent support. Yet significant numbers of less needy households receive support (Joint Center for Housing Studies 2006).

With general income support, given in connection with the tax system or the earned income tax credit (EITC), it would be straightforward to allocate this money in a way that approximates a reasonable horizontal equity standard. With in-kind rental assistance, on the other hand, it would require an enormous increase in expenditures (so all needy families could get decent rental spaces) to bring about a reasonable level of horizontal equity.

A third reason is more subtle, known as the cumulative tax problem. Typical low-income rent programs have families paying 30 percent of their income in rent. This seems fair and appropriate, but there is another way of looking at it. Were the family's monthly income to rise by $100, it would be required pay $30 more in rent, hence sacrificing this $30 and only retaining $70. Programs for food stamps, child care, and other services work essentially the same way. In addition, the family likely pays some Social Security and federal and state income taxes on the increase in income.

When a family benefits from many of these programs, each of which reduces benefits as income increases, these subsidy reductions cumulate into a large effective tax on the family's new income. As the family's income rises, it can sacrifice much or all of its added income in program benefit reductions. Carasso and Steuerle (2005) examine typical families with children whose income rises from $10,000 to $40,000. If they merely participate in universally available programs without queues (earned income credits, food stamps, Medicaid, etc.), they lose about 59 percent of that additional income back to the government in the form of reduced benefits and increased taxes. But if they also participate in housing and welfare programs like Temporary Assistance for Needy Families, they lose about 89 cents out of every additional dollar earned.

This cumulative "tax" seems unfair, and it greatly limits the incentive for the family to earn more income. Replacing various in-kind programs with a general income support program could lessen the difficulties.

There are two contrary arguments in favor of in-kind support. First, general income support can be in terms that congressional decisionmakers do not really understand. For example, what is it really like to live on

$18,000 a year, the cutoff line for the first income quintile? Members of Congress designing an EITC may not have much idea; members of Congress actually observing people in squalid housing and designing in-kind subsidies may have a better idea of just what this support level entails. Further, in-kind support can be better tailored to local price differences than national income support programs. The second argument involves assurance about how the money is spent. In some households, in-kind support will more likely accrue to the benefit of all household members, including children, whereas cash can be spent mainly to benefit the persons getting the checks.

While not all the arguments point in the same direction, there are still strong grounds for converting at least some of the present rental assistance programs to generalized income support programs or programs that are not so restricted, good by good, or service by service. There may not be much difference between the two approaches if the subsidy is thin, but even then there could be a problem involving cumulative benefit reductions. In this case, the general income support approach should always be at least slightly preferable.

Demand-Side Assistance versus Supply-Side Assistance

A second dimension on which programs can be analyzed is whether they support tenants on the demand side of the market or proprietors of rental housing projects on the supply side. Historically most outright expenditures have been supply-side subsidies, with some movement to demand-side subsidies in the 1980s and 1990s. However, as noted, the LIHTC is now growing faster (or declining less slowly) than demand-side subsidies, and rental housing tax expenditures are still supply-side subsidies.

In the simplest economic theory it does not matter whether support is given on the demand or the supply side—the subsidy level to support the desired housing consumption is the same either way. But in more realistic situations, it could matter. Again, there are many arguments for shifting over to more demand-side support. One reason is consumer choice. With demand-side support, tenants can take their voucher (or their general income support) and find the best housing for their needs. They do not have their housing choices constrained by having to live in a particular eligible structure, and they can spend more than their housing voucher if they want. With general income support, they could even spend less than the housing voucher.

A second reason involves what are known as indivisibilities. Many rental structures are large, with a great number of living units. There might be a certain minimum supply-side subsidy necessary to make the project economically viable; below that, it may not be viable. Supply-side support may have to be at least that generous to affect the supply of rental housing at all. Demand-side subsidies can be divided into as many pieces as needed, a gain in horizontal equity if budgets are tight.

A third argument for demand-side support is to avoid graft and corruption. Problems with public housing payoffs have not been epidemic in America, but they have cropped up from time to time, often associated with public housing projects. Giving smaller and more regular assistance on the demand side of the market avoids the temptations implicit in large payments to developers of particular properties. It also takes advantage of the fact that suppliers must remain competitive to keep their renters.

There is at least one counterargument for supply-side subsidies, but it is quite tricky. It involves the fact that the supply of available rental housing in an area is likely to be relatively fixed, constrained by the available land for housing, zoning, or some other factors. Inelastic supply makes it difficult for both demand- and supply-side subsidies. In the simplest theory demand-side subsidies will just push up rents without raising overall supply. Supply-side subsidies will not raise overall supply either: the subsidized units will just displace the unsubsidized units, with no increase in overall supply.

But that is in the simplest theory. In a more complicated world, targeted supply-side subsidies could expand supply. One possibility is that supply-side programs could force the replacement of blighted buildings with better buildings. Overall supply may not increase, but the quality of the housing stock could increase. Supply-side subsidies could improve the location of particular housing projects, nearer to jobs or shopping malls. Or, projects could be negotiated, with the developers agreeing to provide more low-income housing in their structures, a phenomenon known as inclusionary zoning. Each of these instances gets into the finer details of the housing project—it may be that the overall supply is fixed, but there may be targeted supply-side techniques for assuring that low- and moderate-income households get broader housing choices.[3]

Community-based organizations can also add to the value received by lower-income beneficiaries, and they sometimes are successful in inducing higher-income communities to maintain a stock of more modest cost housing. Even when demand-side subsidies are available, efforts have to be made to insure that the communities have owners who will accept them—which often translate closely to supply-side interventions in communities to maintain pockets or shares of new units for moderate-income households.

Before getting too enamored of these possibilities, it should be recognized that the history of supply-side housing subsidies is not very favorable. This history began with large subsidies for enormous public-housing projects that became crime ridden and dilapidated in the 1950s and 1960s. The large public housing projects are a thing of the past, but many of today's supply-side subsidies still have problems, often constraining households to live in certain neighborhoods that are unsafe and where the schools are not good, or that are located far away from the family's place of employment.

The upshot is that while most housing analysts still have a general preference for demand-side subsidies, it is at least conceivable that there could be some role for specially targeted subsidies on the supply side.

Expenditures versus Tax Expenditures

Support for rental housing could also be given on the expenditure side of the budget or the tax side, in the form of tax expenditures such as the LIHTC. The main argument for giving support in the form of explicit expenditures is one of good government. Budgetary expenditures for housing and other types of spending are reviewed annually as part of the budget process. Program analysts must defend the program before congressional critics by showing that it is achieving its objectives. On the other hand, tax expenditures benefiting rental housing or anything else are part of the tax code and are rarely subject to any analysis or questioning.

Tax expenditures result in what are known as tax distortions—allocations of resources that are based on the tax code alone. Whether resource reallocations caused by the tax code are proper or are misallocations depends on underlying social judgments. For projects supported by the LIHTC, there are some areas with adequate supplies of rental housing where the tax inducements may not even be necessary. There are other areas where supplies of rental housing may not be adequate, but where the particular subsidized structures are in poor neighborhoods or in neighborhoods without easy access to jobs. Some distortions introduced into the tax code by the LIHTC may be undesirable. Either way, it is probably better to have these distortions reviewed annually—or at least regularly—as they would be if they were on the expenditure side of the budget.[4]

Federal versus State and Local

A final dimension on which support programs can be analyzed is the federal dimension. Should programs be run out of Washington, D.C., the state capital, or the local government?

Most Depression-era housing programs in the United States were federally financed, such as the FHA and the early public housing programs. Domestic programs in general have often evolved in a shared direction, with the federal government giving matching grants to states or localities, which actually run the programs. This devolution to states and localities has happened in the housing area to a degree, with the CDBG and the HOME programs, and with the LIHTC being administered by state governments.

But there is still a sense in which the governmental roles could be further sorted out. Typically it makes sense for the federal government to concern itself with the underlying distribution of income, to avoid state tax competition for rich households and against poor households. At the same time, it typically makes sense to give states and localities more local control of their areas, involving zoning and general community development. Local conditions differ widely in a large country like the United States, and there is no way that uniform policies adopted in Washington can address highly diverse local situations.

Beyond that, in a federal system states and localities are typically the labs for experimentation and innovation. One state or locality tries something, it works, and the innovations can spread around the system. This does appear to be happening in the housing area. Many states are now introducing innovative policies, and it makes sense to give them more freedom, and more resources, to promote desirable rental housing outcomes. This type of sorting out of roles could avoid having the federal government and the states work at cross-purposes, as sometimes happens now.

In summary, several issues must be considered concerning rental housing programs. Should programs focus more on general income support and less on specific in-kind support? Should programs be more on the demand side and less on the supply side? Should there be more or less emphasis on expenditures or tax expenditures? Should housing programs try to force the federal and state and local governments to better sort out their roles?

A New Approach

Many authorities on housing programs have taken stock recently and argued for fairly radical change in the structure of the nation's housing programs. One frequent object of criticism is the supply subsidies, which may be either inefficient or unnecessary. Another is the scattershot pattern of support, where some low-income households get high support and others none, and where support is tied to living in particular structures in undesirable areas.

Edgar Olsen and John Weicher have looked at these problems and argue for demand-side housing voucher subsidies (Olsen and Tebbs 2006; Weicher 1997). As pointed out above, if these subsidies are thin, demand-side subsidies may in the end be little different from general income support. F. Stevens Redburn (2006) argues for ways to integrate housing support with other social services. John Quigley (2006) argues for improving the horizontal equity of support levels, by switching housing support over to general income support administered in connection with the tax code. On the other hand, William Apgar (1990) makes a rare dissent in favor of supply-side subsidies, arguing that they can be useful in some instances.

The most thorough proposal for revising rental housing programs comes from Margery Austin Turner and Bruce Katz (2006). They follow the demand-side adherents in suggesting conversion of demand subsidies to general income support, say by expanding the EITC.[5] Turner and Katz would also reform the LIHTC to try to eliminate unnecessary tax subsidies given to states without particular housing shortages. They would leave in place the special needs programs for the elderly, disabled, and homeless.

But the main thrust of the Turner-Katz proposal is in the federalism area. They argue for a fundamental change in roles, with the federal government basically confining its activities to income support and the states and localities basically taking over supply-side responsibilities.

Turner and Katz would take advantage of existing metropolitan planning organizations (MPOs) to organize state and local support. These MPOs would have the responsibility of planning housing and community development support within regional areas. Ideally these community development plans would be coordinated with transportation plans, to make sure residents could get to work, and with other infrastructure planning.

The decentralization approach could have various desirable outcomes. It could deal with the fact that demand-supply conditions are different in different areas, and that a one-size-fits-all approach to subsidies may not be sensible. The MPOs might have a better chance at negotiating specially targeted supply-side provisions with developers, to actually increase the supply of housing available to low- and moderate-income households. It is hard to imagine national programs ever dealing with these complexities, but going to the state or MPO level could encourage diverse responses that are tailored to local needs.

There could also be various carrots and sticks to promote desirable outcomes. One carrot could be a competitive grant program, where the MPOs would have to compete to show feasible and attractive plans. If the conflicting responsibilities of overlapping local jurisdictions were to impede progress, as often happens now, there would at least be a procedure for resolving the issues, often not the case now. The same would be true if local zoning regulations were working at cross-purposes with housing goals.

The Turner-Katz proposal does not come with hard and fast budgetary totals, but it is possible to devise a budget-neutral form of their proposal. Referring to tables 3.1 and 3.2, Turner and Katz could improve targeting of the LIHTC and either save some funds, or reallocate funds from states and localities without affordable housing shortages to areas of shortage. They could retain the special needs housing outlays for the homeless, elderly, and disabled. They might convert most or all tenant-based rental assistance, already a demand-side subsidy, to general income support and use it to expand the EITC.

The most complicated issue is to finance the supply-side changes. Turner and Katz could use the present $7.4 billion in existing block grants for this purpose. They could also devote some or all of the $15.1 billion of present federal supply-side assistance into grants to the MPOs. In the short run a portion of these funds may have to be used to honor expiring commitments to proprietors of rental structures. But in the long run the hope is that most present-day subsidies could be could be moved around in the form of competitive grants or other techniques to encourage and permit the MPOs to deal creatively with community development issues, whether on the demand or the supply side.

There could also be some general expansions in rent-subsidy assistance. The high cost of owning or renting in certain jurisdictions would provide an argument.

But there is another factor. If there is a major foreclosure problem in the subprime market, house prices are likely to begin falling. For current owners, this is a bad thing, making it more difficult to refinance high-cost loans. But for renters and other nonhomeowners, the lower prices will lead to a more affordable low-income housing stock. Ironically, some of the present-day affordability problems could be ameliorated by problems in the subprime mortgage market.

Rent-to-Own Options

Rental housing is typically viewed as an alternative to ownership, but in recent years HUD has been promoting a number of programs to marry the two. The central element is to take existing rental programs and to convert some tenants' rent payments to an escrow account to promote homeownership. In contrast to the private subprime market discussed in earlier chapters, where vulnerable borrowers are at the mercy of shrewd lenders, this time the ownership is managed. Tenants build up down payment monies in an account, but they are not actually permitted to buy homes until completing a rigorous counseling program and satisfying other conditions.

One possibility along these lines is in connection with the Section 8 program, a demand-side housing voucher. Beginning in 2000, HUD has permitted local public housing authorities to apply their vouchers toward ownership, through the voucher homeownership (VHO) program. At this point 500 public housing authorities have completed nearly 8,000 voucher-to-ownership conversions, a large share of them with the assistance of NWA.

While admittedly the scale is small, the early experience with the VHO program has been very promising. The VHO purchasers have been mostly female heads of households with children, and mostly minorities. Initially these purchasers had very few assets of their own, and they were forced to take out mortgages with loan-to-value ratios of close to 100 percent, implying virtually no down payment. They received a great deal of counseling before becoming homeowners, and the counseling seemed to have worked: despite the low down payments, foreclosure rates within the

VHO program are only 4 percent. Most VHO participants are successfully building wealth, though starting from a very low home equity base (HUD 2006).

Another option, sanctioned by Congress in 1990, is what is known as the Family Self-Sufficiency (FSS) program. Under this plan, tenant households are required to work with a social service coordinator to form a personal plan that will lead to self-sufficiency. Some of their rent payments go into an escrow account. As long as the family stays in assisted housing, the family can use its escrow account to buy a home, pursue postsecondary education, or start a business. If the family leaves assisted housing, the family can use its escrow account for any purpose. The program can be structured in various ways: all the family's rent could go in the escrow account, giving the maximum benefit for the family, or some could, letting the public housing authority capture some of the gains as tenant incomes rise.

As of yet, the FSS program has not been formally evaluated, but early results are again very positive. Participants seem to be increasing earnings by a large amount compared with nonparticipants. About half of these participants have accumulated sizable escrow balances, and about a third have already become homeowners (Lubell 2006).

These two programs are done at a tiny scale, given the housing needs of millions of low- and moderate-income homeowners. But their initial results are very promising. Should these results hold up, rental housing may someday be viewed less as an alternative to homeowning and more as a potential pathway to successful homeownership.[6]

Manufactured Housing

A different approach, of much greater quantitative importance, involves manufactured housing, the modern term for mobile homes. These have been around for decades, but there has been renewed interest in recent years.

Manufactured homes are factory-built homes, built on a permanent chassis and then transported to their sites using removable axles and wheels. Beginning with the Federal Manufactured Housing Construction and Safety Standards Act of 1974, all manufactured homes must satisfy a standard national HUD examination. Building units in the factory is estimated to cut costs by about 40 percent; even after the expenses of moving the home onto a site, manufactured homes typically cost 20 percent less than site-built units. In an era when house price appreciations are making low-income housing less affordable, there is an obvious reason for the new interest in manufactured housing (Apgar et al. 2002).

Manufactured homes can be located on sites purchased by the homeowner, in which case manufactured housing is for all intents and purposes similar to a normal single-family home. Or manufactured homes can be located on sites owned by an investor, where the investor provides the sewer hookups and other facilities. In this case manufactured housing is a hybrid, where the structure is owned and the land is rented. There are a number of complications with this arrangement, but it also seems to be getting less common. In recent years almost two-thirds of newly installed manufactured homes have been sited on owner-land, and the overall share located on owner-land is now just over half.

For normal single-family homes, most real capital gains (over and above inflation) in effect accrue to the land. The structure can be replicated, but the land cannot, and capital gains essentially reflect the scarcity value of the land. Similarly, when manufactured homes are placed on land owned by the homeowner, capital gains have been roughly as large as with other types of site-built housing. But when manufactured homes are placed on investor-owned land, any capital gains would be only on the structure, and the structure can easily be replicated with new construction. Hence capital gains for structures on investor-owned land have been minimal (Apgar et al. 2002).

The financing of manufactured housing is similar to that in the subprime mortgage market, with a few twists. Most manufactured homes are shipped to dealers and dealers typically provide the financing, operating in a manner similar to the mortgage brokers in the subprime loan market. Owners buying just the home and not the land are eligible for what are called chattel loans, secured only by the structure. Owners buying the whole package can get full mortgages. As with subprime loans, manufactured housing loans have been riskier than conventional mortgages, and the normal APR is 3 or 4 points above the prime mortgage rate. Unfortunately, manufactured housing loans are also susceptible to default, with default rates currently on the order of 12 percent (Apgar et al. 2002).

Manufactured housing has become an important housing option in rural areas, especially the south. The industry typically does well where large multifamily rental structures are rare. Manufactured housing now makes up 16 percent of the rural housing stock, as opposed to only 6 percent in metropolitan areas. Since the mid-1990s, manufactured housing has constituted one-sixth of the growth in the owner-occupied stock overall, one-quarter of the growth in the stock for the lowest income quintile, and growing shares for racial minorities. Since manufactured housing is technically owned, it is considered part of the homeownership sector. Without manufactured homes, the overall United States ownership rate would be lower by 3 percentage points, dropping from 69 to 66 percent.

As with much of the subprime market, manufactured housing has grown privately, though there have been important governmental steps to facilitate the process. The 1974 HUD standards were important in helping establish overall conventions for the industry. The Manufactured Housing Improvement Act of 2000, which clarified tenants' rights against landowners and procedures for resolving disputes, did likewise. And, in recent years HUD has included manufacturing housing targets in the goals set for Fannie Mae and Freddie Mac—now these institutions have to purchase a certain share of manufactured housing loans. For the general mortgage markets it may not make so much sense anymore to have quantitative market share targets for Fannie Mae and Freddie Mac, but for the evolving manufactured housing market this approach seems to have worked.

There is no question that manufactured housing represents a potential answer to some of the nation's affordable housing issues. It has grown rapidly in recent years, and it already represents a significant share of the housing market for low- and moderate-income households and for racial minorities. But before the sector can really take off, some issues must be addressed. Tenants on investor-owned land need stronger protections against interruptions in services. Credit markets need to develop further— for example, it is still virtually impossible to refinance manufactured housing loans. Some of RESPA's settlement procedures should be extended to manufactured housing. There should be better counseling and other services to try to bring down the disturbingly high foreclosure rates. And local housing authorities might think harder about using manufactured housing more intensively in urban areas.

Conclusion

The collapse of several subprime lenders will almost inevitably reverberate on the rental side of the housing market. Rental markets have always been very important in America; there are enough families whose basic needs or family circumstances make it advantageous to rent that this market will always be with us. Right now, about 34 million households in America rent, a number that is not declining even with the recent burst in home-ownership rates. In some sense, a strong rental market is a precondition for a strong ownership market.

But even without any new shake-up in the housing market, there are significant problems with rental housing. There are overall economic issues relating to affordability, there are housing supply problems, and there are spatial location problems.

But there are ways to restructure programs, there are promising new policy approaches that merge renting and owning homes, and there is an interesting new option called manufactured housing. The nation definitely has rental housing challenges, but it also has interesting ways of meeting these challenges. And meeting these challenges is likely to be important in setting the conditions for ownership and as part of a longer-term solution to problems made apparent by the collapse of some subprime lenders.

4

Benefits, Costs, and Risks for the New Homeowners

Owning a home did not get to be the American dream by accident. Society has long felt that homeownership is responsible for all kinds of virtues: homeowners save more; invest more in their children, properties, and neighborhoods; and build more wealth than their counterparts in rental housing. Such feelings could partly explain the many advantages the income tax code bestows on homeowners, even though these tax advantages are probably not very important in the subprime mortgage market. Owners also avoid some of the risks of renting, including dependence on the whims of the rental property owners about tenure and future increases in rent payments.

Whatever the underlying benefits of homeownership in general, any empirical generalizations would be based on past gains in ownership, to households that would have qualified for prime mortgage treatment. The burst in homeownership that began in 1994 focused on different households and a different part of the mortgage market, and earlier results may not be as relevant.

This chapter tries to assess the experiences of the new homeowners. It begins by reviewing the benefits of homeownership in general, and the relevance of these results to the new homeowners of the late 1990s. It then looks at these new homeowners more directly, considering their housing situation, the characteristics of the new mortgages, and the foreclosure process. These analyses are buttressed with a detailed examination of the same variables in the Federal Reserve's Survey of Consumer Finances (SCF), and with a simulation study of potential economic, health, and family shocks.

The Benefits of Homeownership in General

The literature on the benefits of homeownership in general is voluminous. Indeed, at this point there are a great number of surveys of this literature. One of the most complete is provided by Robert D. Dietz and Donald R. Haurin (2003). This section follows their treatment.

The basic virtues of homeownership are alleged to be supported by econometric research. But much of the original research making these claims has a problem known to social scientists as selection bias. Basically, it is hard to tell what comes first, homeownership or the innate preferences and behaviors of those who become homeowners. Do the new homeowners do better because they are homeowners, or because they have greater innate preferences and behaviors and would have done better anyway, regardless of whether they owned a home? The earlier econometric research that found big benefits to homeownership did not deal with this fundamental causation issue.

Beginning about 1990, econometricians started using micro data from surveys and panel studies to try to correct for the selection bias problem. There are two basic ways of doing this. The less elaborate approach is to come up with independent variables to control for the innate preferences and behaviors of the household, and then to measure the gains from homeownership while holding constant these variables. The more elaborate approach is to construct an instrumental variable that predicts homeownership, and then to use that to hold constant the impact of other factors. While neither technique for making this correction is perfect, the studies that make corrections find much smaller impacts of the underlying advantages of homeownership.

Table 4.1 summarizes the results of a large number of studies of homeownership, all based on micro data, all with corrections for the selection bias problem, all using controls, and all done after 1990 (Dietz and Haurin 2003).

From a theoretical perspective, homeowners might be expected to save more than nonhomeowners, because they have what is known as the self-control device of having to make their mortgage payments. There is empir-

Table 4.1. Theoretical and Empirical Impact of Homeownership

Impact on	Theoretical impact	Empirical confirmation
Household saving	Positive	Weak
Wealth accumulation	Strong positive	Strong, if house prices rise
Property improvements	Strong positive	Weak
Urban environment	Strong positive	Weak
Political activity	Strong positive	Strong, on voting
Crime	Strong negative	Weak
Child outcomes	Strong positive	Strong
Satisfaction	Positive	Reasonable
Mobility	Strong negative	Strong
Labor supply	Positive	Reasonable, for women

Source: Author's calculations based on Dietz and Haurin (2003).

ical confirmation of this relationship from survey data, but it is rather weak. Homeowners might be expected to build more wealth, both because of any added saving and the fact that home prices often rise at greater rates than other prices. It turns out that in areas where home prices rise more rapidly than other prices, homeowners do build wealth in their houses, but when home price gains do not outpace other prices, homeowners do not build wealth more rapidly than nonhomeowners. This finding may also reflect the weak and uncertain impact of homeownership on saving.

As for other aspects of investment, homeowners might be expected to try to protect their asset by investing more in their home, neighborhood, and children, or to guard more against crime. There is empirical confirmation of some of these relationships, though not all. There is only weak empirical evidence that crime rates decline. The results are much stronger for investing in children, both their education and their health status. There is also empirical evidence that homeowners are more satisfied than nonhomeowners, though it remains challenging to come up with good empirical measures of satisfaction.

Homeowners might be expected to be less mobile than nonhome-owners, because of the high fixed costs of buying a home. Here there seems to be strong empirical confirmation of this hypothesis. Home-owners clearly stay in their houses longer than renters stay in their places. Homeowners might be expected to work harder, particularly if they have to stretch to make their mortgage payments. There is strong empirical confirmation that at least women in homeowning households increase their number of hours in the paid labor force. Often men have the type of job that prevents marginal adjustment—both their hours worked and their overtime pay may be independent of their homeowner status.

Looking at all the post-1990 studies, there is strong empirical evidence on the mobility issue, and reasonably strong empirical evidence on women's labor supply, voting, satisfaction, and child outcomes. But even for these studies, the measurement of the concept could be suspect (satisfaction), or the relationship between the variable and the concept is remote (voting). Putting all of this together, one can still make a solid empirical case that homeownership carries great benefits for households, but the empirical case is weaker than is commonly believed.

But this case pertains to homeowners in general. What in fact happened in the late 1990s is that the gains and losses of homeownership were extended to a new set of first-time homebuyers. Perhaps the results carry over to this new set of homebuyers, perhaps not. The next section looks at the question in more detail.

The New Homeowners

Christopher Herbert and Eric Belsky (2006) use the American Housing Surveys (AHS) from 1991 through 2003 to take a very careful look at first-time homebuyers. The AHS is an extensive national survey of homebuyers conducted every two years. From 500,000 to 750,000 homebuyers in these years were first-time homebuyers, yielding a very rich source of data on both the physical and financial characteristics of these new homebuyers. In general, these first-time homebuyers are younger than average, have lower incomes, and are more likely to be either black or Hispanic.

Relevant data from the Herbert-Belsky study are given in table 4.2. The first group of variables refers to physical differences between the homes bought by first-time homebuyers and the national average of all households. There has been a worry that these first-time homebuyers would buy dilapidated structures that would not wear well, would need large maintenance expenditures, and might soon become slums. In fact, any physical differences between these houses and all other houses are small. First-time homebuyers have slightly fewer square feet per occupant than the national average, but also slightly newer houses. The share of their housing rated as

Table 4.2. First-Time Homeowners Compared with All Households (percent, except where noted)

	First-Time Homeowners			
	Low income	Moderate income	High income	All households
Physical Characteristics of Home				
Square feet per occupant	545	570	652	662
Built 1970 or earlier	49.7	47.4	40.2	53.4
Moderately or severely inadequate	10.1	9.5	9.5	10.2
Owner Satisfaction (on a 1–10 scale)				
Housing satisfaction	8.1	8.3	8.4	8.1
Neighborhood satisfaction	8.0	8.2	8.2	8.0
Cost Burden, 1995–2003				
Less than 30%	46.3	78.4	93.1	71.5
30–50%	33.5	19.1	6.2	16.0
More than 50%	20.1	2.4	0.6	12.4

Source: American Housing Survey tabulations by Herbert and Belsky (2006).

Note: Cost burden is the amount of the household's disposable income that goes toward housing costs.

moderately or severely inadequate is less than the national average, and the housing physical-satisfaction index is generally above the national average, both for the house and the neighborhood.

There are more grounds for concern when we turn to cost burdens. House prices have risen sharply in recent years, and it is getting harder for households to live cheaply, whether they own or rent. In fact, the first-time homebuyers are not living very cheaply. More than 20 percent of low-income first-time homebuyers have serious cost burdens, defined as spending more than 50 percent of household disposable income on housing. The national average of households with serious cost burdens is 12 percent. The share of low-income first-time homebuyers with moderate cost burdens, spending from 30 to 50 percent of household disposable income on housing, is also much greater than the national average. But while these cost burdens for low-income households are well above average, they are actually below those measured earlier from the American Community Surveys and those that will subsequently be reported by the SCF.[1]

The cost burdens of low-income households that rent are also serious. Indeed, there is little to choose between the two—tabulations from the American Community Survey indicate that 57 percent of low-income renters face serious cost burdens, against 45 percent of low-income owners (Joint Center for Housing Studies 2006). But while both numbers are high and even alarming, the interpretation of these numbers is uncertain.

Basically, the issue is whether interest costs and rent costs are comparable. Renters pay high rent costs and low interest costs; owners, just the reverse. The relative dangers inherent in the two situations would seem to depend on the cost of not making these high payments. For renters, that cost is eviction—renters who do not pay their rent must move, but they will typically not lose many assets. For owners, the cost is foreclosure. Again, those who cannot make their mortgage payments will get evicted and have to move, but this time they could lose their main asset as well. They may also suffer blemishes on their credit reports for as long as 10 years. Accordingly, it would seem that high interest costs are more dangerous than high rental costs. It would also seem that to have such high shares of first-time low-income homebuyers paying more than half their income in mortgage interest costs is an alarming number.

Table 4.3 takes a more complete look at the mortgage situation of these first-time homebuyers. There is nothing dramatic in the interest rates they face—low-income households pay slightly more than higher-income households, but only by a few basis points. Whites pay less than nonwhites, but again, only by a few basis points.

Table 4.3. Mortgage Characteristics of First-Time Homebuyers by Income and Race, 1995–2003 (percent)

	Income Level			Race	
	Low	Moderate	High	White	Nonwhite
Average interest rate	7.43	7.39	7.24	7.38	7.49
Loan-value ratio					
Less than 80%	44.1	38.7	46.6	44.1	38.2
80% to 90%	18.1	23.1	24.4	23.3	18.3
90% to 95%	12.9	14.8	13.7	13.3	16.4
Above 95%	25.0	23.4	15.3	19.3	26.9

Source: American Housing Survey tabulations by Herbert and Belsky (2006).

There is, however, a difference in loan-to-value ratios. Only 44 percent of low-income households have equity in their homes of more than 20 percent (or a loan-to-value ratio of less than 80 percent). And only 38 percent of minority households have equity of more than 20 percent. On the other side, 25 percent of low-income households and 27 percent of minority households have virtually no equity in their home, or a loan-to-value ratio of more than 95 percent. These groups are somehow not paying very high interest rates, but a great many of them are stretched to their financial limits, with virtually no equity in their houses.

One more thing to note about table 4.3 is that while potential mortgage problems seem worse for households with low incomes, these problems are by no means confined to low-income households. For example, while 25 percent of low-income households have little or no equity in their homes, 15 percent of high-income households are in the same position. If and when problems occur, a number of low-income households could get caught, but it should not be surprising if a number of high-income households get caught as well.

But of all the data, perhaps the most worrisome fact about low-income first-time homebuyers does not come from the AHS at all, but from a longitudinal data source called the Panel Survey of Income Dynamics (PSID). This survey follows people over time and finds that 53 percent of low-income first-time homebuyers leave homeownership within five years of buying their first house, compared with 23 percent of high-income buyers. Of course there will always be mobility even among homebuyers—jobs change, families break up, and so forth—but 53 percent seems an incredibly high number. If we take the high-income rate, 23 percent, as a proxy for normal mobility, something like 30 percent of low-income first-time homebuyers may be getting into trouble soon after they buy their house and are being forced to sell.[2]

There are other disturbing facts. As noted earlier, overall personal saving rates are close to all-time lows, and consumer debt burdens and personal bankruptcies near all-time highs (Fellowes 2006). All in a world where housing markets at times suffer from real asset value stagnation or decline. About 40 percent of all homebuyers leave homeowning at some point after buying. It is true that many of these eventually go back to homeowning, but 40 percent also seems a very high number for housing, which is supposed to be a stepping-stone for building wealth. Another fact, again from the PSID, is that the variance of income seems to have increased from earlier decades (Hacker 2006).

The New Mortgages

To get further insight on potential problems within the subprime mortgage market, we now take a more careful look at actual mortgages. First, consider the share of mortgage loans either 60 days delinquent or in foreclosure status, according to Mortgage Bankers Association (MBA) data. Prime mortgage foreclosure rates have been below 1 percent for some years. The FHA foreclosure rate would be expected to be higher, because FHA mortgages are for first-time homebuyers who cannot get prime credit. This FHA foreclosure rate has risen slowly toward 7 percent, but is not likely to rise much in the future because most FHA mortgages are long-term fixed-rate mortgages.

Subprime foreclosures in the MBA data seem to be on a par with FHA foreclosures, but there are two ways in which the MBA numbers for subprime mortgages could be misleading guides to the current and future situation. First, as has been discussed, since subprime loans are predominantly ARMs, there could be large payment shocks as short-term rates readjust. Second, a large share of outstanding subprime mortgages originated in 2005 and 2006, and many of them have not yet matured to the point where problems could occur.

A recent, massive examination of 6 million recently originated subprime mortgages by the Center for Responsible Lending tries to deal with both these issues (Schloemer et al. 2006). Figure 4.1 gives the situation for these mortgages, according to CRL. Subprime mortgages made in 1998, by now largely either prepaid or in foreclosure, seem to have a final completed foreclosure rate of about 8 percent, already higher than the rate in the MBA numbers but not as high as in subsequent years. The presumptive reason for the relatively good performance of these 1998 mortgages is that for most of this time horizon it has been possible for borrowers to sell their houses with reasonable gains and not have to go into foreclosure.

But things get gradually worse. Foreclosures for the 1999 subprime mortgages are above the 1998 numbers, coming in with a final completed foreclosure rate of nearly 11 percent. Foreclosures for the 2000 subprime mortgages are up again and should have a completed foreclosure rate of about 14 percent. Foreclosures in the early stages of a loan (0–40 months) for the next two years are close to the 2000 numbers. But the 2005 and 2006 foreclosure rates are likely to be up again. Using a complicated model that incorporates national house price forecasts, CRL predicts that about 19 percent of the 2005 and 2006 mortgages will eventually foreclose.[3]

Figure 4.1. Subprime Cumulative Foreclosure Rates

Year of origination

☑ Foreclosed after 20 months   ☐ Foreclosed after 20–40 months
■ Foreclosed after 40–60 months   ■ Foreclosed after 60–80 months

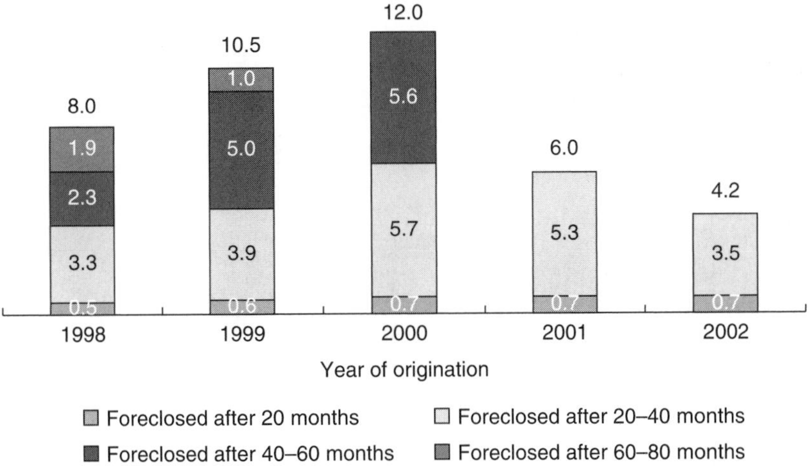

Source: Schloemer et al. (2006).

Notes: Total foreclosure rates reported here underestimate the cumulative foreclosure rates of subprime loans in these origination years. Foreclosures occurring in subsequent 20-month periods were excluded when foreclosure data were not available for all 20 subsequent months.

The aggregate loss of housing equity forecast by CRL due to foreclosures over this period is $164 billion.

But that is not the only problem. As can be seen from figure 4.2, another 5 to 10 percent of these mortgages have been prepaid in distress, with the house selling just before foreclosure. The best indicator of the true debt problem might be the sum of the foreclosure rate and the distress prepayment rate. Given the lower projected rise in house prices, distress sales may decline some, but CRL still estimates that this true debt problem rate on new subprime mortgages could approach 25 percent (Schloemer et al. 2006).

Some of these foreclosures and distress prepayments have already happened, some are forecast. Of course, it is possible that things will turn out better than the CRL forecasts, perhaps because economic conditions might change. But it is also possible that outcomes could be worse. One factor that may make things worse is a decline in the real value of housing in some markets after a long period of extended and usual rise—a problem that could be compounded if interest rates increase.

Figure 4.2. Subprime Loans by Year of Origination

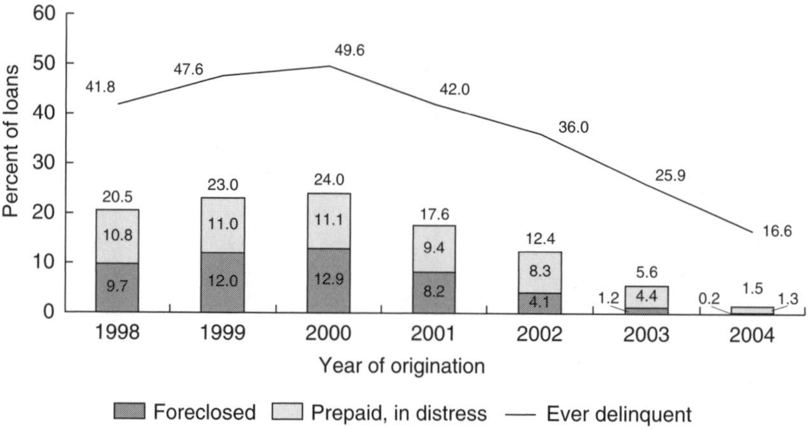

Source: Schloemer et al. (2006).

One factor that may improve things, discussed in other chapters, is the effective intervention of some foreclosure-prevention groups that are now organizing and are already saving many mortgages from foreclosure. Housing purchased at least a few years ago may also have enough past appreciation to withstand a future period of depreciation. So the worst may not happen. But even if it does not, the subprime foreclosure problem could be said to be rising to very damaging levels.

Foreclosures

The foreclosure process also merits a closer look. For this examination, the data come from the Home Ownership Preservation Initiative referred to in chapter 2 and a recently organized national telephone counseling service for delinquent borrowers called the Homeownership Preservation Foundation, or HPF (Homeownership Preservation Foundation 2007). These services take complaints and go to work when they hear borrowers are becoming delinquent in their loan payments, a first step in the foreclosure process. This section focuses on these delinquency statistics.

The first question is what mortgage products seem to get borrowers in trouble. The CRL list includes all the usual suspects. The prevalence of

ARMs, as opposed to fixed-rate mortgages, leads to a much-increased risk. Payment shocks, particularly balloon payments, lead to a much-increased risk. Prepayment penalties lead to a much-increased risk. Loans with no documentation of the borrowers' ability to repay, known on the street as "liar loans," lead to a much-increased risk. And the failure of lenders to create escrow accounts for property taxes and hazard insurance leads to much-increased risk (Schloemer et al. 2006).

Other subprime experts have other candidates. One that often shows up as a predatory or unfair practice is mandatory arbitration. For other loans or contracts, disputes are sometimes resolved with mandatory arbitration, sometimes with negotiated settlements. It may not seem mandatory arbitration would load the dice one way or the other, but since it removes the possibility of bringing class-action suits, lawyers for low- and moderate-income families feel that going to mandatory arbitration puts them at a definite disadvantage.

HPF has kept track of the loan-types where the borrower enters into a mortgage-debt counseling program. The results, in table 4.4, suggest a fairly even split between fixed and adjustable rate mortgages, nearly 40 percent apiece. While these results suggest that ARMs do not cause particular problems, it should be remembered that roughly 80 percent of outstanding mortgage loans are fixed-rate, so in some sense the delinquency problem is four times as great for ARM-type products.

The counseling services also give data on why borrowers get in trouble, shown for the HOPI program in figure 4.3 (the results sum to more than

Table 4.4. Types of Loans in Counseling (percent)

Type	Annual percentage rate	Share
Fixed rate	FHA	5
	Under 8%	21
	Over 8%	15
Adjustable rate	FHA	1
	Under 8%	14
	Over 8%	23
Other[a]		8
Don't know		16

Source: Homeownership Preservation Foundation.

a. Primarily interest only and 80/20 loans. Total exceeds 100 percent because of multiple answers.

Figure 4.3. Causes of Delinquency

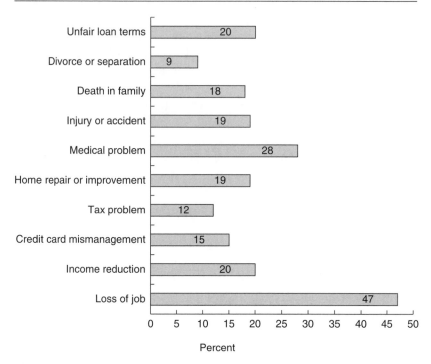

Source: Home Ownership Preservation Initiative data.
Note: Total exceeds 100 percent because of multiple answers.

100 percent because of multiple answers). The most important factor is economic—either job loss (47 percent of respondents) or income reduction (20 percent). Health problems, either medical (28 percent) or injury or accident (19 percent), account for a significant share of delinquencies. Other issues, such as unfair loan terms, home repair problems, credit card problems, divorce, and down the list are important, but not as important as economic and health issues.

Finally, both HOPI and HPF track how they handle complaints. The figures are shown in figure 4.4. In general, if the counseling services hear of problems early, they can take steps to reorganize the loan or refer the borrowers to other support agencies. Perhaps the most difficult issue in fighting foreclosures is to get households that are falling behind on their mortgage payments to come in for help before it is too late. The natural

Figure 4.4. Resolution of Counseling (percent)

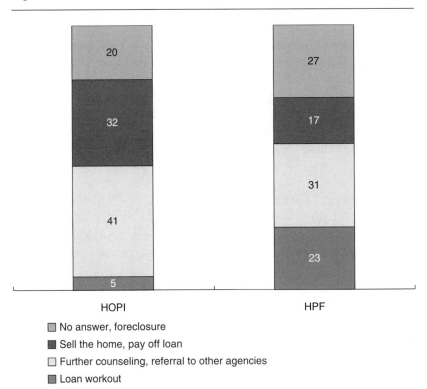

HOPI   HPF

- No answer, foreclosure
- Sell the home, pay off loan
- Further counseling, referral to other agencies
- Loan workout

Sources: Home Ownership Preservation Initiative (HOPI) and Homeownership Preservation Foundation (HPF) data.

human tendency for these households is to worry in silence, but worrying in silence is exactly the wrong approach.

On the numbers themselves, between 17 percent (HPF) and 32 percent (HOPI) of the time the counseling services are able to sell the house, make the prepayment penalty, and unwind the transaction without further loss. About half the time the services are able to negotiate debt workouts or refer the households to other social service agencies in their area. But often— 20 percent of the time for HOPI and 27 percent of the time for HPF— even if the counseling services hear of problems on time, the problems are so insurmountable that the services cannot do anything and the household will probably go to foreclosure.

The latter seems regrettable, but we should keep things in perspective. The big news in figure 4.4 is not that between 20 and 27 percent of troubled borrowers go into foreclosure. It is that between 73 and 80 percent of troubled borrowers do *not* go into foreclosure. We do not know how many of these troubled borrowers would have averted foreclosure in the absence of helpful intervention, but this still seems a remarkable success rate.

There are two important lessons. First, counseling services can make a huge difference, possibly saving up to three-quarters of potential foreclosures. Second, to be most effective, troubled borrowers should go to the services early—there are many more options that way.

The Survey of Consumer Finances

All these inferences are based on outside data, from the American Housing Survey, the CRL loan analysis, or the counseling services. Many results can be cross-checked with data from the SCF, a data series on household wealth compiled by the Federal Reserve.

The SCF is a triennial interview survey of American families, concentrating on families' saving and wealth-building behavior. There are questions about income and health status, but the main focus is on saving and asset questions—did families save, did they invest in assets, what assets, did they take out debt, did they fall behind in their debt payments, and so forth (Bucks, Kennickell, and Moore 2006).

The SCF contains data on about 4,500 respondent households for 1995, 1998, 2001, and 2004—17,565 households in all. In addition to a standard geographically based random sample of the population, the SCF has a special oversample of wealthy families, who loom large in asset accumulation in America. Because of this oversampling, about 60 percent of the households are in the first four income quintiles and 40 percent are in the upper income quintile. Sample weights are used to replicate national averages.

While the survey is periodic, the SCF is not a longitudinal data survey because different households are interviewed in each wave. There is a trade-off between the added costs of following particular households over time and the richness of the survey at each point in time. The SCF has chosen to focus on the richness of the sample and questions.

Basic data from the SCF, with all ratios and quintile breakpoints determined from the weighted data, are shown in table 4.5.[4] The quintile breakpoints are set to replicate overall national numbers, and they will surprise

Table 4.5. Basic Facts from the 2004 Survey of Consumer Finances

Group	Number in sample	Homeowners	Nonhomeowners	Ownership rate (%)	Income brackets (2004 $)
All	17,565	11,769	5,796	67.0	—
1st quintile	2,608	1,035	1,573	39.7	< 18,000
2nd quintile	2,574	1,459	1,115	56.7	18,000–32,000
3rd quintile	2,691	1,795	896	66.7	32,000–52,000
4th quintile	2,827	2,278	549	80.6	52,000–86,000
5th quintile	6,865	6,268	597	91.3	> 86,000
Whites	14,044	10,294	3,750	73.3	—
1st quintile	1,523	739	784	48.5	< 18,000
2nd quintile	1,832	1,145	687	62.5	18,000–32,000
3rd quintile	2,076	1,478	598	71.2	32,000–52,000
4th quintile	2,332	1,929	403	82.7	52,000–86,000
5th quintile	6,281	5,785	496	92.1	> 86,000
Nonwhites/Hispanics	3,521	1,680	1,841	47.7	—
1st quintile	1,085	291	794	26.8	< 18,000
2nd quintile	742	312	430	42.1	18,000–32,000
3rd quintile	615	319	296	51.9	32,000–52,000
4th quintile	495	351	144	70.9	52,000–86,000
5th quintile	584	499	85	85.4	> 86,000

Source: Survey of Consumer Finances (SCF).

Notes: Ratios and breakpoints are based on weighted data. The SCF oversamples wealthy households. The weights adjust for this oversample. The SCF also has an elaborate approach for filling in missing data, where it gives five randomly chosen estimates for the missing data. Standard errors must adjust for this. "Whites" refers to white, non-Hispanic households. "Nonwhites/Hispanics" refers to black households and Hispanic households of any race.

readers unused to data such as these: 20 percent of households have $18,000 of annual income or less (in 2004 dollars) and fall into the first quintile, $32,000 of annual income defines the top of the second quintile, $52,000 of annual income the top of the third, and $86,000 of annual income the breakpoint between the fourth and the fifth (or highest). In terms of the opening up of the mortgage market, there have been big gains in homeownership through the first four quintiles, and some gains in the fifth quintile.

The weighted average homeownership rate in the SCF is 67 percent, very close to the national average from other data sources over this period. The rate for whites averages 73 percent and nonwhites and Hispanics 48 percent, again close to what is obtained from other national data. These homeownership rate differences have been much studied, and are certainly related to the nation's history of racial discrimination. While it is complicated to identify discrimination precisely, a first step is to control for other differences between the races, such as income differences. This can be accomplished by comparing homeownership rates within particular income quintiles. Even quintile ownership rates show significant disparities: 49 percent for whites versus 27 percent for nonwhites and Hispanics in the first quintile, 63 percent versus 42 percent in the second, 71 percent versus 52 percent in the third, 83 percent versus 71 percent in the fourth, and 92 percent versus 85 percent in the fifth.

The main interest is to use the SCF to discern the impact of home-ownership. A first attempt to do that is given in table 4.6. For each income quintile, the table shows the average of the variable for homeowners, non-homeowners, and the difference. The four dependent variables are those that, on preliminary examination, seem to best reflect the underlying benefits and costs of homeownership:

- saving measures the share of households who report some saving out of last year's income;
- net worth gives the total financial and nonfinancial net worth of the household (most of which is the result of its home equity);
- total debts gives the liabilities of the household (again, mainly its mortgage debt); and
- high debt gives a commonly used measure of debt problems—the share of households with monthly debt payments exceeding 40 percent of the household's monthly income (Bucks et al. 2006).

Table 4.6. Mean of Weighted Data of Entire Sample of the 2004 Survey of Consumer Finances

Group	Saving (%)	Net worth ($)	Total debts ($)	High debt (%)
All homeowners	63.2	523,063	84,137	12.2
All nonhomeowners	43.3	54,153	9,942	3.3
Difference	19.9	468,910	74,195	8.9
1st quintile, homeowners	36.0	137,689	18,382	26.0
1st quintile, nonhomeowners	29.1	9,531	3,591	6.3
Difference	6.9	128,158	14,791	19.7
2nd quintile, homeowners	50.9	184,641	32,388	20.4
2nd quintile, nonhomeowners	40.8	25,234	7,344	2.2
Difference	10.1	159,407	25,044	18.2
3rd quintile, homeowners	59.2	217,867	57,432	15.0
3rd quintile, nonhomeowners	52.9	45,816	12,494	1.7
Difference	6.3	172,051	44,938	13.3
4th quintile, homeowners	70.8	316,419	87,277	8.0
4th quintile, nonhomeowners	62.8	96,672	16,984	0.9
Difference	8.0	219,747	70,293	7.1
5th quintile, homeowners	78.7	1,306,477	161,643	2.9
5th quintile, nonhomeowners	74.9	442,166	41,240	0.2
Difference	3.8	864,311	120,403	2.7

Source: SCF.

Results from the table are straightforward. Homeowners do save more than nonhomeowners, 63 percent for homeowners versus 43 percent for nonhomeowners. But as with the racial disparities, homeowners in general have higher incomes than nonhomeowners; hence, it is not surprising that the saving disparities within income quintiles are smaller, ranging between 4 and 10 percentage points. Homeowners have a great deal more net worth, especially in the fifth quintile. This too is not at all surprising, given that the SCF was administered in a time of generally rapidly rising home prices.

Homeowners have more debt than nonhomeowners, reflecting the well-known fact that in order to have a chance at capital gains, owner-investors are likely to have to take on debt and take a chance. Accompanying these higher overall debt levels is a much higher share of homeowner households with high debt burdens, according to the standard measure. This time the overall disparity is 9 percentage points, but within the quintiles the disparities range from 20 percentage points in the first quintile to 3 percentage points in the fifth quintile.

Three tables in the appendix deal with obvious questions about table 4.6. Table 4A.1 removes those households where the head is over age 65 from the sample, to avoid problems of interpretation involving retired families with low incomes and very high net worth. As expected, this change cuts some of the high-income net worth disparities, though not the disparity in the first quintile. Curiously, it strengthens the disparities for the share of households with high debt costs. But in other respects the changes from eliminating households with heads over age 65 are minor.

Tables 4A.2 and 4A.3 show results separately for white and nonwhite and Hispanic households, again with the head age 65 or younger. As might be expected, net worth builds up less rapidly for nonwhite and Hispanic households, presumably because they are not able to buy houses in markets that appreciate in value as rapidly as are white households. Within income quintiles, nonwhite and Hispanic households only have higher debt costs than whites in the third and fourth income quintiles, not the lower quintiles or the highest quintile.

But as argued above, the best way to analyze these data is to run regressions where a host of outside factors can be controlled. In addition to the factors mentioned already, these regressions have controlled for the interview wave of the household, marriage status, history of filing for bankruptcy, negative income shocks, and negative health shocks. The results for the impact of homeownership on the four dependent variables, in weighted regressions with all household heads 65 or less, shown separately for the different races, are given in table 4.7.

The table contains two sets of numbers, the first a regression coefficient measuring the impact of homeownership on the relevant dependent variable, and the second the difference in means. For all variables but net worth, the two estimates are reasonably close. With net worth, the means can be unduly influenced by a handful of households that may have received enormous capital gains—here the fitted regression coefficients give much more reliable estimates of the likely impact on households.

The underlying results give much the same impressions as those already discussed. Homeowners seem clearly to save more, from 8 to 10 percent

Table 4.7. Regression Coefficients and Weighted Sample Means by Income Quintile, Head Age 65 or Younger

IMPACT OF HOMEOWNERSHIP ON

	Saving (%)		Net Worth ($000)		Total Debt ($000)		High Debt (%)	
	Regression coefficient	Difference in means	Regression coefficient	Difference in means	Regression coefficient	Difference in means	Regression coefficient	Difference in means
White Households and Nonwhite and Hispanic Households								
White Households								
1st quintile	8.0	6.1	120	150	31	28	39.6	34.9
2nd quintile	9.2	9.0	80	136	44	38	30.4	26.3
3rd quintile	2.6	2.9	67	132	57	52	13.7	13.4
4th quintile	6.0	5.8	99	170	86	75	7.2	6.5
5th quintile	1.4	1.1	360	783	127	127	3.2	2.6
Nonwhite/Hispanic Households								
1st quintile	9.8	6.4	88	93	23	23	36.1	34.4
2nd quintile	4.9	0.2	61	67	43	41	29.9	28.2
3rd quintile	6.0	5.5	65	79	70	65	23.1	23.4
4th quintile	6.1	7.9	103	148	96	93	12.6	13.3
5th quintile	8.6	10.6	201	463	117	141	4.3	4.5

Source: SCF.

Note: "White" refers to white, non-Hispanic households. "Nonwhite/Hispanic" refers to black households and Hispanic households of any race.

more in the first quintile to lesser numbers in the top quintile. But even in the top quintile, the saving disparities for minorities are significant.

Also on the positive side, homeowners seem clearly to have accumulated more wealth, by amounts in the neighborhood of $100,000 for the first four quintiles, and much more than that in the top quintile. These homeowners have gotten this equity by taking on more debt, by amounts that gradually increment across the quintiles for both races. In this case, there are minimal racial differences within income quintiles for the degree to which homeowners have taken on debt.

But that brings up the danger signal. Again using the standard measure of troublesome exposure to debt—the share of households having monthly debt service payments exceeding 40 percent of monthly income—homeowners are clearly in worse shape. As discussed above, the direction of this result is not at all surprising. Nonhomeowners will typically have much less debt, and much higher rent payments. But the quantitative magnitudes suggested by table 4.7 are disturbing.

To investigate these magnitudes, it is helpful to go back to means again, as is done in figure 4.5. Because renters are irrelevant to this comparison, the figure focuses exclusively on owners, giving the absolute level of the high-debt rate for owners. These range from 43 percent of first-quintile

Figure 4.5. High-Debt Households by Income and Race

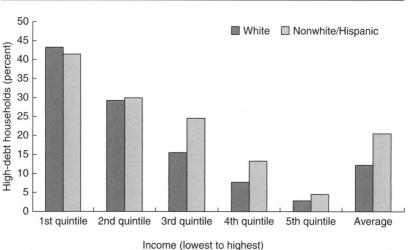

Income (lowest to highest)

Source: 2004 Survey of Consumer Finances.

Notes: Means are weighted. All heads of households are age 65 or younger.

whites to 3 percent of fifth-quintile whites, averaging 12 percent for the whole white homeowner population. The rates range from 41 percent of first-quintile blacks and Hispanics to 5 percent of fifth-quintile blacks and Hispanics, averaging 21 percent for the whole nonwhite owner population. High-debt rates average 14 percent for the entire homeowning population. These numbers are much as reported in the American Community Surveys, significantly above those from the American Housing Survey, as reported earlier (Joint Center for Housing Studies 2006, table A-6). Clearly a very high share of the population, from different races and ethnicities and virtually all income levels, has very high debt burdens and is at risk of potential foreclosure problems.

It should be emphasized that there do seem to be potential, and sizable, wealth gains for homeownership, particularly when house prices rise rapidly. But these same households have often taken on very high debt levels to achieve these gains, and they are vulnerable to shocks in their income or health status. In addition to asking whether homeownership in general is a desirable proposition for certain types of families, it is important to determine these families' vulnerability to adverse shocks in their income or health status.

Simulation Results

This vulnerability can be investigated with the aid of a simulation model. The Urban Institute's Dynasim model is ideally structured to answer the questions.[5]

Beginning with the results in figure 4.5, the simulation confined the population to homeowners with heads younger than age 65. It created ten groups of such households, two racial/ethnic groups (whites and nonwhites) and five income groups for each racial/ethnic category. For each of these ten groups the simulation randomly allocated debt burden problems according to the ratios in the figure: 43 percent of low-income white households had randomly allocated debt burden problems, 29 percent of second-quintile white households had randomly allocated debt burden problems, and so forth.

The data were then subjected to the shock routines of Dynasim. Each family was subjected to the Dynasim probabilities of income, health, and marriage shocks from 2003 to 2007. Income shocks were defined as income falling 20 percent from the previous year in any of the four years. Health shocks were defined as the onset of an injury or disability limiting the household head's ability to work in any of the four years. Marriage shocks were defined as dissolution of the marriage in any of the four years. The last category was the union of these sets—any of the three types of shocks in any of the four years.

The results of the procedure are given in table 4.8. Of the 43 percent of first-quintile white homeowners with high debt burdens, 61 percent are likely to suffer a negative income shock sometime in a four-year period, 6 percent a health shock, 3 percent a marriage shock, and 65 percent at least one of the three shocks. Similar numbers can be traced along the appropriate row of the table. In general, these shock probabilities are reasonably low for health and marriage status, but very high for income status, essentially in line with the PSID results that the variance of family income over time seems to be high and getting higher (Hacker 2006). Even upper-income families are vulnerable to some shock or other over a four-year period, particularly an income shock. If the family begins with a very high debt burden, as 12–13 percent of homeowning families do, there is roughly an 80 percent chance of a significant adverse shock from one of these three sources.

Table 4.8. Probability of Adverse Shock in Four Years by Income Quintile, 2003–07

Shock	1st quintile	2nd quintile	3rd quintile	4th quintile	5th quintile
White					
Income	61.3	80.0	84.2	81.9	88.2
Health	6.3	4.2	5.0	7.2	5.9
Marriage	3.4	4.2	6.3	7.2	5.9
Any of above	64.8	81.9	86.1	84.3	91.2
Nonwhite/Hispanic					
Income	57.5	71.4	77.0	80.7	74.6
Health	5.3	5.9	6.7	6.4	3.5
Marriage	3.8	4.9	7.0	4.9	7.0
Any of above	61.1	74.8	80.6	83.4	78.9

Source: Urban Institute Dynasim Model.

Notes: Sample is all debt-burdened, homeowning families where the head is age 65 or younger. "White" refers to white, non-Hispanic households. "Nonwhite/Hispanic" refers to black households and Hispanic households of any race.

Of course, many families can weather this shock and still make their mortgage payments. And some will get opposing positive shocks. But many cannot weather the shock, and as more families get stretched to the limit to make their debt payments, the likelihood of adverse income or health shocks in turn makes foreclosures more likely.

Conclusion

The bottom line here is straightforward. The recent boom in home-ownership has put many families in the position of being able to accumulate greater wealth through their houses. It has also burdened a large number of families—about 40 percent in the lowest income quintile and 12 percent overall—with very high debt loads. Given income instability, it becomes highly likely that at some point these families will suffer a significant income loss and have significant problems making their mortgage payments.

There is a big difference between falling behind on a mortgage and actually getting foreclosed. But if a homeowner who falls behind does not take positive action, a foreclosure becomes very likely. There are counseling groups out there to help, and these groups are averting foreclosures for many households. But many households have high debt burdens, many of them are likely to suffer adverse shocks, and many are at risk of foreclosure. These problems are worse for low-income households, but even high-income households are vulnerable. And market conditions could get much worse because of the additional risks added by the bubble in housing prices from the late 1990s to the early 21st century.

With the collapse of various subprime lenders, one of the nation's primary goals over the next few years should be the avoidance of a domino effect that forces large and unnecessary losses on households through unnecessary or premature foreclosures. Another should be the maintenance of a viable mortgage market for many moderate-income households, but one that imposes fewer risks than the one just preceding it. I turn now to these topics.

Appendix Tables

Table 4A.1. Mean of Weighted Data, 2004 Survey of Consumer Finances (Household Heads Age 65 or Younger)

Group	Saving (%)	Net worth ($)	Total debts ($)	High debt (%)
All homeowners	64.9	493,875	103,573	13.8
All nonhomeowners	44.6	47,083	10,849	3.7
Difference	20.3	446,792	92,724	10.1
1st quintile, homeowners	36.8	139,023	31,189	42.6
1st quintile, nonhomeowners	30.2	7,559	4,317	7.6
Difference	6.6	131,464	26,872	35.0
2nd quintile, homeowners	48.2	138,057	46,809	29.4
2nd quintile, nonhomeowners	40.7	18,613	7,875	2.4
Difference	7.5	119,444	38,934	27.0
3rd quintile, homeowners	57.2	160,425	68,662	17.4
3rd quintile, nonhomeowners	52.5	38,012	13,033	1.8
Difference	4.7	122,413	55,629	15.6
4th quintile, homeowners	70.2	255,584	96,433	8.7
4th quintile, nonhomeowners	63.1	84,533	17,325	0.9
Difference	7.1	171,051	79,108	7.8
5th quintile, homeowners	78.3	1,127,036	170,773	3.1
5th quintile, nonhomeowners	74.8	363,153	40,137	0.2
Difference	3.5	763,883	130,636	2.9

Source: Survey of Consumer Finances.

Table 4A.2. Mean of Weighted Data, 2004 Survey of Consumer Finances (White Households, Heads Age 65 or Younger)

Group	Saving (%)	Net worth ($)	Total debts ($)	High debt (%)
All homeowners	67.2	553,804	106,359	12.2
All nonhomeowners	49.2	64,721	13,707	3.7
Difference	18.0	489,083	92,652	8.5
1st quintile, homeowners	37.4	159,616	33,916	43.2
1st quintile, nonhomeowners	31.3	9,725	5,863	8.3
Difference	6.1	149,891	28,053	34.9
2nd quintile, homeowners	52.1	159,574	46,940	29.2
2nd quintile, nonhomeowners	43.1	22,857	9,233	2.9
Difference	9.0	136,717	37,707	26.3
3rd quintile, homeowners	58.8	173,620	66,696	15.5
3rd quintile, nonhomeowners	55.9	41,151	14,491	2.1
Difference	2.9	132,469	52,205	13.4
4th quintile, homeowners	72.0	268,159	94,444	7.7
4th quintile, nonhomeowners	66.2	98,609	19,091	1.2
Difference	5.8	169,550	75,353	6.5
5th quintile, homeowners	78.6	1,199,205	171,033	2.8
5th quintile, nonhomeowners	77.5	415,902	43,737	0.2
Difference	1.1	783,303	127,296	2.6

Source: Survey of Consumer Finances.

Note: "White" refers to white, non-Hispanic households.

Table 4A.3. Mean of Weighted Data, 2004 Survey of Consumer Finances (Nonwhite and Hispanic Households, Heads Age 65 or Younger)

Group	Saving (%)	Net worth ($)	Total debts ($)	High debt (%)
All homeowners	55.2	242,290	91,874	20.5
All nonhomeowners	37.9	21,675	6,731	3.7
Difference	17.3	220,615	85,143	16.8
1st quintile, homeowners	35.6	99,057	25,897	41.4
1st quintile, nonhomeowners	29.2	5,641	2,948	7.0
Difference	6.4	93,416	22,949	34.4
2nd quintile, homeowners	37.5	79,766	46,454	29.9
2nd quintile, nonhomeowners	37.3	12,572	5,942	1.7
Difference	0.2	67,194	40,512	28.2
3rd quintile, homeowners	51.5	111,204	75,993	24.5
3rd quintile, nonhomeowners	46.0	32,058	10,266	1.1
Difference	5.5	79,146	65,727	23.4
4th quintile, homeowners	63.1	196,179	105,829	13.3
4th quintile, nonhomeowners	55.2	48,357	12,785	0.0
Difference	7.9	147,822	93,044	13.3
5th quintile, homeowners	76.2	646,898	169,044	4.5
5th quintile, nonhomeowners	65.6	184,018	27,912	0.0
Difference	10.6	462,880	141,132	4.5

Source: Survey of Consumer Finances.

Note: "Nonwhite and Hispanic" refers to black households and Hispanic households of any race.

5

Policy Changes

I t is tempting to treat the opening of the subprime mortgage market, and the concomitant increase in homeowning rates, as a social experiment to be evaluated. Of the roughly 12 million new homeowners, this share of the new homeowners has gained a certain amount and that share has lost a certain amount, leading to an overall social tally.

But that is not a very helpful way to look at things. Realistically, the nation cannot go back to the starting point. The subprime market came about through a series of changes, these changes are difficult to reverse, and it would not even make sense to reverse most of them. The subprime market is here to stay, and American homeownership rates are probably permanently higher by up to 5 percentage points. The task rather should be to see if policy changes could improve the social balance, lessening either the cost or likelihood of foreclosures while preserving the gains in wealth building that have taken place. This chapter takes that approach.

New Approaches Involving the Rental Market

The first issue is to assure an adequate supply of rental housing, a necessary concomitant to a healthy market for homeownership. This issue was discussed in chapter 3, and three types of changes were recommended. The most important was a redesign of rental subsidies along the lines of Turner and Katz to improve the efficiency of the LIHTC, convert much of present demand-side assistance to general income support, and devolve much or all of present grants and supply-side assistance to states and localities. Specifically, the Turner-Katz proposal would create local metropolitan planning organizations to handle the generalized community development needs for particular areas. The MPOs could determine the appropriate mix of demand- and supply-side subsidies in their area, negotiate any targeted supply-side subsidies, and determine housing needs along with community development and transportation needs.

A difficult aspect of this change is to get the right mix between demand-side and targeted supply-side subsidies. While determining this mix is highly complex, the job should probably be left to the MPOs because local conditions are of fundamental importance. These local conditions vary widely from jurisdiction to jurisdiction, and only the MPOs would seem to have a chance at determining the best approach for a particular jurisdiction. Certainly it is impossible to see how this could be done at the national level.

In addition, effective supply-side subsidy approaches will often have to be negotiated with local developers. The MPOs will have the community knowledge and the continuing relationships with developers. Again, it is almost impossible to imagine how this could be done at any level of government other than the local level.

Apart from structure, a big question here is whether to expand the overall supply of rental housing. The answer would seem to be yes—many communities have intense affordability issues, and supply expansion would make sense.

But another factor bears consideration. The foreclosure problem, discussed at length in other chapters, may lead to a downward movement in home values, as suppliers place these foreclosed properties on an already-glutted market. For present homeowners, this is the worst possible news, making it hard to refinance and build equity. But for renters and CBOs just trying to get people in houses, it is the best possible news. In many communities, the downward adjustment in home values may do the work of an expansion in rental supplies.

There are successful rent-to-own projects—at this point done on a very small scale, affecting just thousands of households. The big issue here is to try to take these programs to scale without losing the value of the early experimental programs. It seems renters can learn to become successful homeowners, but the process is not easy. It is necessary to counsel prospective homeowners, combine housing support with other social services, and work out saving devices where some of the rent payments of these households goes into accounts that enable households to accumulate funds for down payments or to build wealth in other ways.

The last issue here is to improve the process for manufactured housing, often a hybrid between owning and renting. For owners of manufactured housing who place their structures on land owned by an outside landlord, some clarifications and improvements of tenant rights may be necessary. At present the Real Estate Settlement Procedures Act does not apply to manufactured housing, and it probably should. The foreclosure rates for manufactured housing are still distressingly high, and the types of measures to be discussed below for subprime lending in general may also be appropriate for manufactured housing.

High-Roads and Low-Roads

Turning now to subprime markets themselves, there is no question that certain practices have to be cleaned up. Some lenders take advantage of borrowers' ignorance, some exploit borrowers, and some are outright predatory.

The subprime market is not the first market to have had problems of this sort, and often suppliers have cleaned up their own act. Duncan Kennedy has raised the provocative question of whether this could happen in the subprime loan market. High-road creditors make money the old-fashioned way, by making loans and earning interest. They lose earning assets when borrowers default. But low-road creditors make money through the foreclosure process. If the high-road creditors could self-enforce practices that strengthen borrowers' rights and lessen foreclosure, they could in theory put low-road creditors out of business, without any government intervention at all (Kennedy 2005).

The idea may seem fanciful, but it is really not. First, the recourse provisions in many sale agreements will naturally force lenders to clean up their own acts. These lenders may have thought that they could just make shaky loans and pass them on—it probably takes about one housing cycle to correct that notion, and we are well into that cycle. In the future, the financial institutions that buy and securitize mortgages will likely enforce much stricter lending standards.

Beyond that, many lenders are trying to avert problems on their own. According to recent press reports, some large subprime lenders, such as

Bank of America and CitiMortgage, are contacting borrowers and offering to restructure mortgages.

In terms of developing standards for "best practices," the Mortgage Brokers Association has already done this, and many state organizations have done likewise. These organizations could also enter into a *Consumer Reports*–type grading of institutions, loan products, brokers, and the like (Apgar and Essene 2007). They could also put in place compliance measures to ensure that all their members follow the guidelines.

Another common approach for self-improvement is disclosure. Just disclose what happened, and relevant institutions will do what has to be done to fix the problem. In line with this, John Makin's approach to fixing up the subprime market is to have the Federal Reserve write a complete report of exactly what went wrong in the recent subprime market cycle (Makin 2007).

There may always be a need for government regulation of the subprime mortgage market, but that need goes down if the industry tries to police itself.

Banning or Making Costly Certain Practices

As for more traditional government regulation, the obvious question is whether there should be more of it. There are already overarching federal statutes discouraging discrimination, insuring proper disclosure, and encouraging banks and thrifts to make loans to low- and moderate-income households. There is also a statute against predatory lending, the Home Owner Equity Protection Act of 1994. Are these statutes enough?

One key to answering this question is HOEPA. While at present HOEPA coverage is minimal, in the past its provisions have been used to lead the subprime market. HOEPA already regulates the high-priced part of the subprime loan market by banning certain practices and making other practices very costly. Practices that are banned are balloon payments, defined as sharp increases in loan payments any time in the first five years of a loan, and prepayment penalties that extend for longer than five years. Practices that are made costly are single-premium credit insurance. HOEPA also requires lenders to verify borrowers' ability to repay a loan, and it forces buyers of HOEPA loans to take legal responsibility for actions of lenders, known as assignee liability.

One possible way to limit the foreclosure problem, and the influence of predatory lenders, is to expand the domain of HOEPA. Certain additional practices could be banned, or the thresholds defining HOEPA loans could be tightened, making HOEPA cover more loans.

Evaluators of the new subprime loans, such as the Center for Responsible Lending, train their focus on six suspect practices. One is the large payment shocks implicit in many 2/28 loans, 3/27 loans, or other ARM-type products. Another is the failure to escrow property taxes and insurance payments, making it likely that borrowers will face unanticipated payments. A third is the long-term prepayment penalties, which make it difficult for borrowers to get out of subprime loans. A fourth is that lenders are not properly assessing and documenting borrowers' ability to repay the loans. A fifth is that borrowers are able to lie about their income, as in liar-loans. The final practice is the yield-spread premiums, which give brokers an incentive to steer borrowers to high-cost lenders.

Many of these practices could be limited by revising HOEPA. To determine whether a loan falls under HOEPA, the APR is computed for the entire term of the loan, the fixed period of 2 years and the adjustable period of 28 years. Hence the mere structure of the 2/28 loan or the 3/27 loan does not get around HOEPA provisions. But the payment shock implicit in these loans is not subject to the balloon payment test. It could be made subject, within the spirit of the law, by extending the provision to any large increase in loan payments—for example, lenders could not increase the APR or monthly payment on a loan by more than, say, 50 percent from one year to the next. Were provisions like this in place, lenders would be reluctant to offer low teaser rates or any other type of ARM loan that entailed a big payment shock. A variant of this approach is that HOEPA could require lenders to make their maximum APR more visible.[1]

As for prepayment penalties, HOEPA could be rewritten to limit the term of the prepayment penalty, either to three years or to the term of the first interest rate (say two years in a 2/28 loan or three in a 3/27 loan). There is an argument that prepayment penalties protect the lender, who is after all making a long-term loan. On the other hand, lenders have already waived virtually all prepayment penalties in the prime mortgage market, and a slight weakening of these penalties in the subprime market does not seem out of order.

The practice of documenting the borrowers' ability to repay the loans is already an important feature of HOEPA. The HOEPA language already requires that lenders consider both current and future income in making this assessment. But a broader concept borrowed from securities law is beginning to get some attention, known as the suitability doctrine. Taken literally, this doctrine requires lenders to make loans that are "suitable" for borrowers, or in the borrowers' best interest. Several states have instituted variants of this suitability doctrine. These statutes have been criticized as too vague to be operational, and it remains to be determined exactly how these suitability standards will be implemented and adjudicated in various states. For the HOEPA segment of the market, it also remains to be determined exactly how the present HOEPA regulations compare with the suitability doctrine (Apgar and Essene 2007).

HOEPA loans already include yield-spread premiums in their APR calculations, a first step in limiting mortgage brokers. It is possible to go a step further and actually limit the yield-spread premiums on HOEPA loans, perhaps to average broker costs. Another way to restrain brokers would be to require lender-paid homeowner counseling for all loans, or to require lenders to pay for second opinions on mortgage contracts.

Finally, HOEPA loans require buyers of loans to take responsibility for problems in the loan process, known as assignee liability. Several members of Congress have proposed broadening the assignee liability process, either on its own or through an expansion of HOEPA.

So while the HOEPA provisions already limit lenders in various ways, expansions are certainly possible. The balloon payment stricture could be extended to any sort of APR increases, or any sort of payment shock. The allowable prepayment penalty period could be reduced. The ability-to-pay provision could be broadened to a suitability test. Counseling and/or second opinions could be required. Assignee liability could be extended.

Another way to extend the domain of HOEPA is to tighten the thresholds so more subprime loans fall under its scope. Right now, after the recent tightening by the Federal Reserve, the 8-percentage point threshold for first-lien loans has put only about 1 percent of all subprime loans under HOEPA (Avery et al. 2006).[2] Tightening the threshold to 5 percentage points should put more loans under HOEPA—about 50 percent of all subprime loans, according to tabulations from HMDA. As before, this estimate may prove high if lenders respond by cutting their rates. Going to a threshold of 3 percentage points would put virtually all subprime loans under HOEPA.[3]

While there is an argument for tightening the HOEPA thresholds, there is also an argument for not going all the way to 3 percentage points. Because of assignee liability, HOEPA loans are already difficult to sell, and any new regulations should not prevent the secondary market efficiencies from being extended to the subprime market. Hence if the HOEPA threshold were left at 5 percentage points, subprime lenders would have the option of pricing loans below the HOEPA threshold, and being able to sell them, or going above the threshold, and being subject to all the added HOEPA borrower protections. The mortgage market in fact already works this way; a partial tightening keeps that mechanism in order while still reducing the number of subprime borrowers forced to go without HOEPA protections.

It is also possible to use a two-tiered approach to HOEPA, as the Federal Reserve already did in its last HOEPA change. Instead of making the HOEPA threshold uniform, either Congress or the Federal Reserve (presumed to continue in charge of the precise regulations) could have a higher threshold for one type of loan than another. In the last round of changes the Fed wanted to discourage unnecessary refinancing of first-lien mortgages, so it lowered the HOEPA threshold on first-lien mortgages and left it unchanged on junior-lien mortgages. In this round, since ARMs have become the main issue, the Fed could leave the threshold alone for fixed-rate mortgages and only lower it for ARMs. Since lenders apparently will go to some lengths to avoid being covered by HOEPA, such a two-tiered approach could be quite powerful and greatly defuse lenders' interest in ARMs. This in turn would assure that many more borrowers get better information about the long-run costs of their mortgages.

In a deeper sense, lowering the HOEPA threshold works in the direction of the old usury laws, tending to close up the subprime market. Do we want to go in this direction?

There are two reasons a partial lowering of the threshold might be an acceptable compromise. Forty states now have their own predatory lending laws, and about 20 of them have already lowered their HOEPA thresholds. A careful study of state lending by Giang Ho and Anthony Pennington-Cross finds that these threshold changes have not materially affected the amount of subprime lending in the affected states. Indeed, Ho and Pennington-Cross even argue that as what they call dishonest lending is closed down, clean subprime lending could increase in the state (Ho and Pennington-Cross 2006).[4]

In addition, expanding the national HOEPA law is economically efficient. As the national law tightens, it replaces and overrides many state predatory lending statutes. Some states will presumably always have their own standards, but more lending will fall under the national regulations, which will be the same from state to state. The "crazy quilt" is in effect replaced by a much more uniform quilt, to the benefit of national lenders.

In this sense, it is more efficient for national lenders to deal with a reasonably binding national law instead of 40 different state laws.

Fannie Mae and Freddie Mac have recently announced that they are considering withdrawing from the subprime market, but a different sort of change could complement HOEPA policies. These two secondary market entities have made a huge difference in securitizing and standardizing the prime mortgage market, but they have been less of a presence in the subprime market. They could evolve into a presence, and they could nicely complement HOEPA, or a tightened HOEPA.

HOEPA bans or makes it costly for lenders to engage in certain practices—balloon payments, long-term prepayment penalties, not documenting the repayment ability of the borrower. But because of assignee liability provision, HOEPA loans are difficult to sell. Fannie Mae and Freddie Mac could operate below the HOEPA thresholds, 8 percentage points now but perhaps going down, and agree to buy these near-high-priced loans, provided that the loans do not contain the same practices that are also penalized in HOEPA (and perhaps some other practices). Under this scheme, lenders could make really high-priced loans that fall under HOEPA and are difficult to sell, and moderately high-priced loans below the HOEPA threshold that Fannie Mae and Freddie Mac would buy. Both types of loans could be expunged of questionable practices, HOEPA by regulation and Fannie-Freddie by the secondary market entities themselves.[5]

In this new regime, market-share targets for Fannie Mae and Freddie Mac would not be the best indicators of success. The two agencies might be highly effective in cleaning up the overall subprime market, but if some lenders do not adhere to the Fannie-Freddie standards, or if other secondary market institutions buy the subprime loans, Fannie and Freddie may not have that many subprime loans actually on their books. The real test of their effectiveness is what happens in the whole subprime market, not how many subprime loans either agency purchases.

There is a final sword in the regulator's sheath. HUD administers RESPA, the statute that sets conventions for determining closing costs and other settlement provisions. These are paid by borrowers at settlement, under RESPA rules that require lenders to give "good faith" estimates of closing costs. Problems ensue when these good-faith estimates prove inaccurate or when they are not given in time to be useful to borrowers. The Government Accountability Office has criticized these disclosures on a number of grounds (U.S. Government Accountability Office 2006).

One approach is to penalize lenders for inaccuracy: another, often preferred by academic economists, is to permit lenders to bundle costs and compete on the overall package—essentially what is done in most other consumer markets (Guttentag 2005). HUD has had various proposals under consideration that have tried to deal with the issues, but these have been the subject of intense lobbying from title firms, and no proposals are currently on the table. Once some of the issues get worked out, there is at least the theoretical possibility that housing costs may be lowered through RESPA reform.

Increasing the Supervision of Lenders and Brokers

We saw in chapter 2 that only 20 percent of subprime lenders face the rigorous examinations faced by commercial banks and thrifts. Another 29 percent of subprime lenders face weaker supervision, sometimes supervised like banks and thrifts but sometimes under a form of indirect supervision, where the parent bank, thrift, or holding company takes responsibility for the actions of the subsidiary or affiliate. And 51 percent of subprime loans are made by state-chartered independent lending companies, not subject to conventional supervision by federal agencies. Since New Century Financial has gone bankrupt, the 51 percent will go down, but the problem is still there.

This hole in the supervisory safety net is both inequitable and economically inefficient. Supervised entities like banks and thrifts are being forced to compete in the subprime market against unsupervised entities. If these unsupervised entities can engage in actions that make business sense, if not social sense, they can win the competitive race. Restoring what is known as a level playing field would involve confronting all subprime lenders with the same supervisory environment.

Were the same set of supervisions extended to all subsidiaries, affiliates, and independent mortgage companies, several current harmful practices could be combated. A long-time staple of banking regulation is that the lender should try to ascertain the repayment ability of the borrower. As CRL points out, today this often does not happen in the subprime market, but it could be made to happen with expanded supervision.

Similarly, the practice of not escrowing for insurance and taxes on subprime loans could be ended, as could the practice of assessing borrower soundness using the short-term ARM teaser rates. In particular, lenders could be forced to evaluate the borrower's ability to pay using the published maximum rate on an ARM, not the short-term teaser rate. Finally, the safety and soundness provisions of normal banking supervision could be extended to the subprime market, particularly to the loans with large implicit payment shocks. These loans are anything but safe and sound, and even if HOEPA itself does not limit or cap the payment shocks, the supervisors of financial lenders could stop the practice.

Increased supervision of subprime lenders would eventually entail the regulators getting down into the details of actual loan transactions with the lenders. This would seem a major change from the present situation, but it would not actually be that difficult to bring about. For some years the nation has had very thorough supervision of most lenders in the prime mortgage market. This supervision has already been extended to those banks and thrifts that participate in the subprime market (constituting 20 percent of total loans). All subsidiaries and affiliates of national banks and thrifts (30 percent of the total) could be brought under the same supervisory conventions as their parents, seemingly without major culture shock. Indeed, some bank regulators, the OCC, OTS, and the Fed are already doing this selectively.

The big issue would be the state-chartered independent mortgage companies, now responsible for half the subprime loans. New regulators would have to be established for these companies. Administratively they are listed in the HUD-supervised category, but the HUD supervisors are not bank regulators, and state supervision typically does not fill the gap either. There are various ways to skin this cat, but somehow or other all subprime lenders should be brought under the tight federal supervision scheme that is now faced by banks and thrifts. This change would require new legislation.

One potential worry that should not be a problem is the budget deficit. For those concerned about deficits, there is no added cost to this supervisory extension. The banking world has the tradition that the supervised entities pay the cost of their own supervision. These entities create the need for the supervision, and they should and do pay for it.

The Role of Community-Based Organizations

The last resort in any attempt to clean up the subprime mortgage market is the behavior of community-based organizations. The low-income housing market is unique for the presence of large, often well-funded, usually effective community-based organizations that watch over lenders and borrowers. Earlier these CBOs were important in breaking down barriers to lending. Nowadays, these barriers are pretty much broken down, but there are still major foreclosure and financial literacy problems. Many CBOs have made impressive efforts in these areas, but of course more can always be done.

One approach is preventive. The Opportunity Finance Network has amassed capital and is going into business as a subprime lender, to compete with private lenders. It is putting the finishing touches on a plan to offer fixed-rate clean subprime mortgages on a large scale throughout the nation. An alternative approach for groups less able to tap into large pools of funds would be to provide automatic pricing guides to loans and lenders, perhaps on a web site. Prospective borrowers could key in their own data and determine the loan terms they might qualify for. There could be enough publicity that it would be more difficult for lenders to exploit borrowers.

But even if the preventive approach does not work, the amelioration approach still could. Previous chapters have detailed the efforts of the Home Ownership Preservation Initiative and the Homeownership Preservation Foundation. Essentially these groups work as counseling services, activated when borrowers report that they are falling behind on their loan payments. These services have hot lines and are able to tap into alternative sources of credit. But they are in some sense at the mercy of borrowers, who often do not speak up in time. Still, these two services have already saved thousands of homes from foreclosure.

The model is out there, and further efforts might save millions of homes, especially if banks step up by contributing some new capital (and getting CRA credits). The federal government could also provide new capital, presumably given through the counseling services. And if community groups can restructure mortgages, why not the FHA-VA? These are government agencies, after all. They too could develop programs to move payment-shock ARM borrowers into long-term fixed-rate mortgages.

Promoting financial literacy is a more long-term approach, but it is every bit as important. Lenders could not take advantage of borrowers, and borrowers would not make as many unwise decisions, if borrowers simply knew more about how financial markets work. Borrowers should understand how interest rates are computed, the difference between money today and money tomorrow, the need to save, and the need to make long-term financial plans. They should realize that lenders do not always have the borrowers' best interest in mind and be able to see through the pitches of manipulative sales personnel. Recent testing of high-school students, even from upper-income districts, finds pretty woeful general knowledge about financial issues; as long as that is true, borrowers are vulnerable.[6]

Financial literacy can never be the whole answer to predatory lending and foreclosure problems. Mortgage contracts are complicated, even for those with advanced degrees in finance.[7] But with more knowledge of finance and literacy comes power: consumers have at least some knowledge of the principles of finance, and some ability to sort out the good advice from the bad. They also realize that apparent free money is really not that, that low payments today may mean high payments tomorrow, and that one has to consider the long-run implications of any financial contract.

There is already a huge effort to promote financial literacy. Each banking agency has a national program, lenders can get CRA credit for literacy programs, and many private vendors are selling literacy programs. But even then, the efforts of the CBOs have been and can be extremely valuable.

Conclusion

The subprime mortgage market has arrived and is here to stay, presumably to cover 20 percent or more of new mortgages in future years. Subprime borrowers have worse credit histories and lower incomes than prime borrowers, and it should be no surprise that they pay a higher price for credit. Higher prices may be acceptable, but these buyers should not be taken advantage of, either by questionable lenders, questionable loans, or by their own questionable decisions.

Tightening up, or cleaning up, subprime mortgage markets requires action from many groups. Many borrowers will have to work harder to understand their transactions. Many lenders will have to work harder to police their own industry or restructure their unviable loans. Many CBOs will have to work harder on financial literacy and foreclosure prevention. And there may be more work for government regulators as well, either in more rigorous supervision of subprime lenders or in expanding the scope of current protective laws. One important issue is to find ways to use the present legal structure to limit the large payment shocks that are now so common in subprime mortgages. Another, of even more importance, is to eliminate the hole in the supervisory safety net.

Notes

1. The New Mortgage Market

1. Recently the Federal Reserve, along with the Federal Deposit Insurance Corporation, the National Credit Union Administration, the Office of the Controller of the Currency, and the Office of Thrift Supervision, felt compelled to put out a guide to the new mortgage products (2006). The Government Accountability Office (GAO) has a parallel piece (2006).

2. See also Board of Governors of the Federal Reserve System (2000).

3. These numbers come from tabulations of the Home Mortgage Disclosure Act (HMDA) data for 2005.

4. Nick Timiraos, "The Subprime Market's Rough Road," *Wall Street Journal*, 17 February 2007.

5. Serena Ng and James R. Hagerty, "Does the Subprime Index Amplify Risk?" *Wall Street Journal*, 27 February 2007. The fund is called the ABX-HE index.

6. The data are given in Fellowes (2006).

7. See Joint Center for Housing Studies (2006). The numbers are computed from the American Community Surveys and given in table A-6, page 36.

2. The Evolution of This Market

1. The figures are from the Federal Reserve, reprinted in the *Economic Report of the President,* all years, table B-75, "Mortgage Debt Outstanding by Type of Property and of Financing."

2. See *Economic Report of the President,* table B-75, "Mortgage Debt Outstanding by Type of Property and of Financing, 1949–2006." Available at http://www.gpoaccess. gov/eop/2007/B75.xls.

3. The figures are from the Federal Reserve, reprinted in the *Economic Report of the President,* all years, table B-76, "Mortgage Debt Outstanding by Holder."

4. Most subprime borrowers likely do not itemize deductions. But if they do, as in the rest of the tax system, subprime mortgage interest and property taxes are also tax deductible.

5. The latest numbers of brokers are taken from *Mortgage Brokers in 2004,* Wholesale Access Mortgage Research and Consulting, July 28, 2005.

6. Mortgage banker numbers for 2006 suggest that the numbers could even be higher.

7. See also Jackson, Berry, and Burlingame (2005).

8. Mason and Rosner (2007) describe this process well.

9. Some of the problems are detailed in Kathleen C. Engel and Patricia A. McCoy, "Turning a Blind Eye: Wall Street Finance of Predatory Lending," mimeo, June 19, 2006.

10. The original Boston Fed article is Munnell et al. (1996). Ladd (1998) summarizes the issues that have turned up during the lengthy debate.

11. Author tabulations from HMDA data.

12. The pre-change numbers are in Gramlich (2002). The post-change numbers are in Avery et al. (2006).

3. Rental Housing

1. A good discussion of these programs can be found in Green and Malpezzi (2003).

2. Calculations from the Joint Center on Housing Studies (2006), page 36.

3. These issues are discussed in Apgar (1990).

4. The jurisdictional problem, however, is not easy to solve. When testifying on the potential relative advantage of demand-side vouchers over the LIHTC in the late 1980s, Deputy Assistant Secretary of the Treasury Eugene Steuerle was addressed by now Chairman of the Ways and Means Committee Charles Rangel (D-NY). Congressman Rangel effectively said that when the Ways and Means Committee had jurisdiction over demand-side subsidies, he would consider the trade-offs, but for now he would get money for lower-income households through the policy instruments under his committee's control—that is, through the tax code.

5. A related proposal was made by Robert Lerman and Eugene Steuerle in a book examining voucher programs in general: the development of a combined voucher that could be spent on a variety of goods or services, including education and housing. See Lerman and Steuerle (2000).

6. One issue in making the conversions involves finding appropriate incentives for local housing authorities to participate and cooperate. Perhaps the MPOs of Turner-Katz will be necessary to make headway on this problem.

4. Benefits, Costs, and Risks for the New Homeowners

1. The earlier numbers were taken from the Joint Center for Housing Studies (2006), table A-6. The later numbers will be described below.

2. See the discussion in Herbert and Belsky (2006).

3. Pennington-Cross and Ho (2006) also find that controlling for house prices, about 18 percent of subprime mortgages are expected to default.

4. The SCF has an unbalanced sample, with disproportionate numbers of high-income households. The weights adjust for this oversampling. The SCF also has a complicated way of filling in missing data. Regressions are run to predict the missing data with other variables, and then these missing observations are filled in with five estimates, chosen randomly from the regression's error distribution. Whenever standard errors are used, one must be sure to count observations properly. Throughout this section, "white" refers to white, non-Hispanic households. "Nonwhite and Hispanic" refers to black households and Hispanic households of any race.

5. Favreault and Smith (2004) describe how the model works.

5. Policy Changes

1. By law, this maximum APR must already be given to borrowers, and the change might simply emphasize the fact. Bucks and Pence (2006) find that while borrowers generally seem to understand their mortgage terms, for one reason or another they do not seem to understand how much their adjustable interest rate could change through a resetting.

2. The 8-percentage-point threshold is the lowest permitted in the HOEPA statute. To lower the threshold would take new legislation. As noted earlier, when the Fed first made the change, it expected that the incidence of HOEPA loans would be much higher.

HOEPA does give the Fed authority to ban certain practices throughout the mortgage market. Up to this point, the Fed has been reluctant to use the authority to clean up the problems in a small segment of the market.

3. Author tabulations from 2005 HMDA data.

4. Ho and Pennington-Cross develop an index of the strength of the HOEPA law in various states, but they do their statistical analysis on otherwise-like counties in states with and without strict HOEPA laws. Their results are at variance with an earlier study that just compares overall state subprime lending. See Elliehausen and Staten (2004).

5. Fannie Mae and Freddie Mac are not actually prevented from buying HOEPA loans. But these loans do not count in meeting the goals HUD sets for the two entities, hence eliminating most of the incentive to buy the loans.

6. Operation Jumpstart coordinates the testing of high school students for financial literacy. On multiple-choice exams where one of four answers is correct (and where a monkey could then score on average about 25 percent), the typical high-school student scores about 45 to 50 percent.

7. In particular, Apgar and Essene (2007) report that in lab experiments even Chicago finance students were often not able to figure out the lowest present-value cost loans.

References

Apgar, William C. 1990. "Which Housing Policy Is Best?" *Housing Policy Debate* 1(1): 1–32.

Apgar, William C., and Ren Essene. 2007. "Understanding Mortgage Market Behavior: Creating Suitable Mortgage Options for All Americans." Discussion paper. Cambridge, MA: Joint Center for Housing Studies, Harvard University.

Apgar, William C., and Allen J. Fishbein. 2005. "Changing Industrial Organization of Housing Finance and Changing Role of Community-Based Organizations." In *Building Assets, Building Credit: Creating Wealth in Low-Income Communities*, edited by Nicolas P. Retsinas and Eric S. Belsky (107–36). Washington, DC: Joint Center for Housing Studies and Brookings Institution Press.

Apgar, William, Allegra Calder, Michael Collins, and Mark Duda. 2002. *An Examination of Manufactured Housing as a Community- and Asset-Building Strategy.* Washington, DC, and Cambridge, MA: Neighborhood Reinvestment Corporation and Joint Center for Housing Studies, Harvard University.

Avery, Robert B., Kenneth P. Brevoort, and Glenn B. Canner. 2006. "Higher-Priced Home Lending and the 2005 HMDA Data." *Federal Reserve Bulletin,* September 8: A123–66.

Benston, George J. 1997. "Discrimination in Mortgage Lending: Why HMDA and CRA Should Be Repealed." *Journal of Retail Banking Services* 19(3).

Board of Governors of the Federal Reserve System. 2000. *The Performance and Profitability of CRA-Related Lending.* Report by the Federal Reserve Board to Congress, July 17.

Bucks, Brian, and Karen Pence. 2006. "Do Borrowers Know Their Mortgage Terms?" Working paper. Washington, DC: The Federal Reserve.

Bucks, Brian K., Arthur B. Kennickell, and Kevin B. Moore. 2006. "Recent Changes in U.S. Family Finances: Evidence from the 2001 and 2004 Survey of Consumer Finances." *Federal Reserve Bulletin,* March 22: A1–38.

Carasso, Adam, and C. Eugene Steuerle. 2005. "The Hefty Penalty on Marriage Facing Many Households with Children." *Future of Children* 15(2): 157–75.

Carasso, Adam, Elizabeth Bell, Edgar O. Olsen, and C. Eugene Steuerle. 2005. "Improving Homeownership among Poor and Moderate-Income Households." Opportunity and Ownership Project Brief 2. Washington, DC: The Urban Institute.

Dietz, Robert D., and Donald R. Haurin. 2003. "The Social and Private Micro-Level Consequences of Homeownership." *Journal of Urban Economics* 54(3): 401–50.

Elliehausen, Gregory, and Michael Staten. 2004. "Regulation of Subprime Mortgage Products: An Analysis of North Carolina's Predatory Lending Law." *Journal of Real Estate Finance and Economics* 29(4): 411–33.

Favreault, Melissa, and Karen Smith. 2004. "A Primer on the Dynamic Simulation of Income Model." *Assessing the New Federalism* Discussion Paper 04-02. Washington, DC: The Urban Institute.

The Federal Reserve, the Federal Deposit Insurance Corporation, the National Credit Union Administration, the Office of Comptroller of the Currency, and the Office of Thrift Supervision. 2006. *Interest-Only Mortgage Payments and Payment-Option ARMs: Are They for You?* Washington, DC: The Federal Reserve.

Fellowes, Matt. 2006. "Credit Scores, Reports, and Getting Ahead in America." Metropolitan Policy Program Survey Series. Washington, DC: The Brookings Institution.

Fishbein, Allen, and Patrick Woodall. 2006. *Exotic or Toxic? An Examination of the Nontraditional Mortgage Market for Consumers and Lenders.* Washington, DC: Consumer Federation of America.

Goldstein, Ira J. 2007. *Lost Values: A Study of Predatory Lending in Philadelphia.* Philadelphia, PA: The Reinvestment Fund.

Gramlich, Edward M. 1999. "A Policy in Lampman's Tradition: The Community Reinvestment Act." *Focus (Institute for Research on Poverty)* 20(3): 11–14.

———. 2002. "Predatory Lending." Speech before the Housing Bureau for Seniors, Ann Arbor, Michigan, January.

Green, Richard K., and Stephen Malpezzi. 2003. *A Primer on U.S. Housing Markets and Housing Policy.* Washington DC: Urban Institute Press.

Guttentag, Jack. 2001. "Another View of Predatory Lending." Working Paper 01-23-B. Philadelphia: Wharton Financial Institutions Center, University of Pennsylvania.

———. 2005. "Reforming the Home Mortgage Market: Attacking the Problem Rather Than Its Symptoms." Working Paper 05-31. Philadelphia: Wharton Financial Institutions Center, University of Pennsylvania.

Hacker, Jacob S. 2006. "Universal Insurance: Enhancing Economic Security to Promote Opportunity." Hamilton Project discussion paper. Washington, DC: The Brookings Institution.

Herbert, Christopher E., and Eric S. Belsky. 2006. *The Homeowner Experience of Low-Income and Minority Families: A Review and Synthesis of the Literature.* Washington, DC: U.S. Department of Housing and Urban Development.

Ho, Giang, and Anthony Pennington-Cross. 2006. "The Impact of Local Predatory Lending Laws on the Flow of Subprime Credit." *Journal of Urban Economics* 60(2): 210–28.

Homeownership Preservation Foundation. 2007. *The Subprime Mortgage Lending Default and Foreclosure Crisis: What Are Incentives for Financing and Supporting More Effective Intermediary Interventions?* Minneapolis, MN: Homeownership Preservation Foundation.

Jackson, Howell, Jeremy Berry, and Laurie Burlingame. 2005. "Kickbacks or Compensation: The Case of Yield Spread Premiums." *Annual Review of Banking.*

Joint Center for Housing Studies, Harvard University. 2006. *The State of the Nation's Housing: 2006.* Cambridge, MA: Joint Center for Housing Studies, Harvard University.

Kennedy, Duncan. 2005. "Cost-Benefit Analysis of Debtor Protection Rules in Subprime Market Default Situations." In *Building Assets, Building Credit: Creating Wealth in Low-Income Communities,* edited by Nicolas P. Retsinas and Eric S. Belsky (266–82). Washington, DC: Brookings Institution Press.

Ladd, Helen F. 1998. "Evidence on Discrimination in Mortgage Lending." *Journal of Economic Perspectives* 12(2): 41–67.

Lerman, Robert I., and C. Eugene Steuerle. 2000. "Structured Choice versus Fragmented Choice: Bundling of Vouchers." In *Vouchers and the Provision of Public Services,* edited by C. Eugene Steuerle, Van Doorn Ooms, George Peterson, and Robert D. Reischauer (471–502). Washington, DC: Brookings Institution Press.

Lubell, Jeffrey. 2006. "Strengthening Resident Opportunities for Self-Sufficiency and Homeownership through Rent Reform Linked to Asset-Building." Washington, DC: Center for Housing Policy.

Makin, John H. 2007. "Risk and Return in Subprime Mortgages." Washington, DC: American Enterprise Institute.

Mason, Joseph R., and Joshua Rosner. 2007. "How Resilient Are Mortgage Backed Securities to Collateralized Debt Obligation Market Disruptions?" Paper presented to the Hudson Institute, Washington, D.C., February 15.

Munnell, Alicia H., Geoffrey M. B. Tootell, Lynne E. Browne, and James McEneaney. 1996. "Mortgage Lending in Boston: Interpreting HMDA Data." *American Economic Review* 86(1): 25–53.

Neighborhood Housing Services of Chicago. 2006. *Partnership Lessons and Results: Home Ownership Preservation Initiative.* Chicago, IL: Neighborhood Housing Services of Chicago.

NeighborWorks America. 2006. *NeighborWorks America and the NeighborWorks Network Annual Report 2005.* Washington, DC: NeighborWorks America.

Office of Management and Budget. 2006a. *Analytical Perspectives, Budget of the United States Government, Fiscal Year 2007.* Washington, DC: U.S. Government Printing Office.

———. 2006b. *Appendix, Budget of the United States Government, Fiscal Year 2007.* Washington, DC: U.S. Government Printing Office.

Olsen, Edgar O., and Jeffrey M. Tebbs. 2006. "The Effect on Program Participation of Replacing Current Low-Income Housing Programs with an Entitlement Housing Voucher Program." Mimeo.

Opportunity Finance Network. 2006. *2005 Annual Report.* Washington, DC: Opportunity Finance Network.

Passmore, Wayne. 2003. "The GSE Implicit Subsidy and Value of Government Ambiguity." Discussion Paper 2003-64. Washington, DC: The Federal Reserve.

Pennington-Cross, Anthony, and Giang Ho. 2006. "The Termination of Subprime Hybrid and Fixed-Rate Mortgages." Working Paper 2006-042A. St. Louis, MO: Federal Reserve Bank of St. Louis.

Quigley, John M. 2006. "Just Suppose: Housing Subsidies for Low-Income Renters." Paper presented at "Revisiting Rental Housing: A National Policy Summit," Cambridge, Mass., November.

Redburn, F. Stevens. 2006. "Rethinking Federal Low-Income Housing Policies." Working paper. Washington, DC: New America Foundation.

Renuart, Elizabeth. 2004. "An Overview of the Predatory Lending Process." *Housing Policy Debate* 15(3): 467–502.

Ross, Steven L., and John Yinger. 2002. *The Color of Credit: Mortgage Discrimination, Research Methodology, and Fair-Lending Enforcement.* Cambridge, MA: MIT Press.

Schloemer, Ellen, Wei Li, Keith Ernst, and Kathleen Keest. 2006. *Losing Ground: Foreclosures in the Subprime Market and Their Cost to Homeowners.* Durham, NC: Center for Responsible Lending.

Turner, Margery Austin, and Bruce Katz. 2006. "Rethinking U.S. Rental Housing Policy." Paper presented at "Revisiting Rental Housing: A National Policy Summit," Cambridge, Mass., November.

Turner, Margery Austin, Todd M. Richardson, and Stephen Ross. 2007. "Housing Discrimination in America: Unequal Treatment of African Americans, Hispanics, Asians, and Native Americans." In *Fragile Rights within Cities: Government, Housing, and Fairness,* edited by John Goering (39–60). Lanham, MD: Rowman and Littlefield Publishers, Inc.

Turner, Margery Austin, Fred Freiberg, Erin Godfrey, Carla Herbig, Diane K. Levy, and Robin R. Smith. 2002. *All Other Things Being Equal: A Paired Testing Study of Mortgage Lending Institutions.* Washington, DC: U.S. Department of Housing and Urban Development.

U.S. Department of Housing and Urban Development. 2006. *Report on the Voucher Homeownership Study.* 2 volumes. Washington, DC: U.S. Department of Housing and Urban Development.

U.S. Government Accountability Office. 2006. *Alternative Mortgage Products: Impact on Defaults Remains Unclear, but Disclosure Risks to Borrowers Could Be Improved.* GAO-06-1021. Washington, DC: U.S. Government Accountability Office.

Weicher, John. 1997. *Privatizing Subsidized Housing.* Washington, DC: AEI Press.

Zigas, Barry, Carol Parry, and Paul Weech. 2002. "The Rise of Subprime Lending: Causes, Implications, and Proposals." Discussion paper. Washington, DC: Fannie Mae.

About the Author

Edward M. Gramlich is the Richard B. Fisher Senior Fellow at the Urban Institute in Washington, D.C. In 2005–06, Dr. Gramlich was interim provost at the University of Michigan. From 1997 to 2005, he was a member of the Board of Governors of the Federal Reserve System. He is the Richard A. Musgrave Collegiate Professor Emeritus of Public Policy and has served as dean of the University of Michigan's School of Public Policy. He also served as chair of the Quadrennial Advisory Council on Social Security, first deputy and then acting director of the Congressional Budget Office, director of the Policy Research Division of the Office of Economic Opportunity, and a senior fellow at the Brookings Institution.

Dr. Gramlich wrote a popular text on benefit-cost analysis that is now in its second edition (*A Guide to Benefit-Cost Analysis,* Waveland Press, 1997). He also wrote *Is It Time to Reform Social Security?* (University of Michigan Press, 1998). His work for the Urban Institute Press includes *The Government We Deserve: Responsive Democracy and Changing Expectations* (edited with C. Eugene Steuerle, Hugh Heclo, and Demetra Smith Nightingale, 1998). His other books and articles cover macroeconomic topics, housing, budget policy, income redistribution, fiscal federalism, and the economics of professional sports.

Index